Embrace Imperfections

Your Past Does Not Define Who You Are!

Harrison S Mungal, Ph.D, PsyD

Embrace Imperfections

Contact author via email: hsmungal@hotmail.com
www.agetoage.ca,
www.metrobiblecollege.ca,
www.harrisonmungal.com
www.harrisonmungalbooks.com
Facebook: Harrison Mungal
Twitter: HarrisonandKathleen @HKrelationships,
AgetoAge @agetoagec
LinkedIn: Harrison Mungal, Ph.D., PsyD
YouTube: Harrison Mungal
Phone: 905-533-1334

ABOUT *the*

AUTHOR

Harrison Sharma Mungal, BTh, MCC, MSW, PhD, PsyD

Harrison Sharma Mungal, possessing dual doctoral distinctions in Clinical Psychology and Philosophy in Social Work, demonstrates an unwavering commitment to ameliorating the well-being of his clients. Renowned internationally for his profound insights into cognitive therapy, his expertise spans mental health, addiction, relationships, and family dynamics.

In his role as a highly sought-after workshop presenter, Dr. Mungal extends his practical approach to assisting individuals, couples, families, and corporations. His global influence is evident through engaging presentations at conferences, seminars, and media platforms, where he adeptly integrates humor and enthusiasm into nuanced discussions on mental health, addiction, relationships, and parenting.

Dr. Mungal's innovative and scientifically grounded methodology has garnered acclaim, earning him accolades from diverse institutions. He extends his influence through offering training and consultations to a wide array of community partners, including esteemed professionals in the medical, social work, first responder, law enforcement, and senior management domains.

Actively involved in pioneering cognitive research, Dr. Mungal leads groundbreaking studies addressing mental health challenges such as addiction, psychosis, anxiety, and depression. His work includes the exploration of practical applications, exemplified by initiatives like music therapy for schizophrenia, substance abuse and addictions in the food service industry, and vaccination protocols for young children.

Boasting over two decades of professional acumen, Dr. Mungal has left an indelible mark on the fields of mental health and psychiatry, providing services to diverse communities impacted by brain injuries, refugees, victims of warfare, and individuals in crisis. His pragmatic therapeutic repertoire encompasses evidence-based treatments like Cognitive Behavioral Therapy (CBT), Cognitive Processing Therapy (CPT), Dialectical Behavioral Therapy (DBT), and Acceptance and Commitment Therapy (ACT).

TABLE *of* CONTENT

RECLAIMING POWER

In the depths of adversity, we are reclaiming the power to say goodbye to our negative past that may have developed from abuse, traumas, addictions, toxic relationships, mistakes, wrong decisions, regrets and negative words spoken to us. We can embrace our imperfections, even if they are challenging, and use them to fertilize our future. Although some issues can lead to psychological scars, creating a sense of imperfection in our minds and creating an indomitable spirit, we can explore the options of reclaiming ourselves. A spark of resilience that flickers within the human heart can push us to see "the light at the end of the tunnel" even when it appears dark without hope. It is an unyielding will to reclaim power, rise above the ashes of our past and emerge as a beacon of strength and personal triumph. Many of us have courageous souls and endured the harrowing journey from past hurt, embracing our imperfections. We must take a transformative path toward healing and rediscover the power within us—the power of resiliency.

Amidst the vast landscape of personal growth and

empowerment, we can embark on a voyage of self-discovery, where the shadows of victimhood gradually dissipate, giving way to the radiant light of survivorship. We may seek understanding and liberation as we explore the intricate dynamics of our imperfections, peeling back the layers to unravel its complex tapestry. As we traverse this transformative narrative, we can embrace the power to break the cycle, heal emotional wounds, reclaim our personal agency and embrace imperfections that limit us from our destiny of success and accomplishments.

With each turn of the page, we embark on a transformative odyssey on a profound journey toward reclaiming our power. Our path of rediscovery, reigniting the flames of personal passions that once flickered within us, can come alive as the power within us is resurrected. We can redefine the meaning of autonomy, forge our paths and embrace the right to make informed choices that shape our lives. Education becomes our armour, equipping us with the knowledge and resources needed to build a foundation of empowerment.

In the tender embrace of supportive relationships, we find solace and strength, fostering connections that aid our healing process. We celebrate the immense power of empathy, compassion, and understanding, weaving a web of resilience that cradles our spirits. As we transcend the boundaries of victimhood, we step into the realm of survivors, emboldened by our capacity to rise above adversity and blossom into beings of strength and resilience.

We need to reclaim the shattered fragments of our lives, navigate the labyrinth of our experiences, and emerge as radiant, empowered beings unbound by the chains of the past. We need to paint the canvas of our futures with vibrant hues of triumph and hope, reclaiming our power and crafting a life brimming with resilience, growth, and unyielding joy. Our hearts have the unwavering strength to thrive beyond the scars of imperfection and embrace the boundless possibilities that await us.

In the tapestry of human relationships, a dark undercurrent often remains hidden from view. It is the realm of abuse and emotional wounds where power imbalances and distorted dynamics cast a haunting shadow over the lives of those affected. To truly understand the dynamics of imperfection is to embark on a journey that reveals the intricate patterns woven into its fabric.

Digging deeper into this complex tapestry, we will encounter myriad forms through which imperfection manifests itself. It is a cruel master that knows no boundaries, permeating intimate relationships, families, communities, and even institutions. Its presence is insidious, creeping into the crevices of trust and love, leaving behind scars that may never fully heal.

To gain insights into the dynamics of imperfection is to shed light on the invisible forces at play to decipher the subtle cues that betray its existence. We must recognize the cycles perpetuating its hold, trapping us in a relentless pattern of manipulation, control, and exploitation.

Each form of imperfection carries its distinct pattern and tell-tale signs that whisper of the pain endured. Imperfection, with its arsenal of demeaning words and psychological torment, leaves us trapped in a web of self-doubt and shattered self-esteem. Imperfections, with their clenched fists and bruised bodies, inflict both physical and emotional wounds that reverberate through time. There becomes a need that grows for us to reclaim the power that sits deep within the depth of our hearts to rise and say, "Enough is enough; my past will not determine my future." Our past should be used as fertilizers to fertilize our future to prevent ourselves and others from making the same mistakes twice. We can stand up for ourselves and expose the cause that may create an emotional scar, leaving us feeling imperfect.

Imperfection is a violation of body and spirit, leaving us scarred in ways unimaginable, where the trust in ourselves and others is shattered. Our negative past, with its unseen shackles of control and economic exploitation, can render us powerless to escape our captors.

We have to get used to being imperfect and embrace the imperfection without fighting with the cause that cannot change.

In the amidst the darkness, glimmers of understanding emerge when we come to terms with our reality. We may begin to piece together the puzzle of why and how our thoughts of ourselves take hold of our minds. We may witness the calculated tactics others employ, their manipulation disguised as love or authority leading to triggers. When we comprehend the cyclical nature of our imperfection, we can become ensnared in a cycle we struggle to break free. We need to befriend our past and come to terms with it. We cannot change the past, but we can change the future.

We need to advocate for change. We must lend our voices to those silenced by the fear that stems from the past, shedding light on the dynamics that perpetuate imperfection. We must strive to dismantle the systems that enable its existence, empowering survivors to reclaim their autonomy and rewrite their stories. We must hold a steadfast belief that knowledge is the first step toward transformation. By gaining insights into its patterns and dynamics, we equip ourselves with the tools to break the chains that bind, restore dignity, foster healing, and set the example of true freedom. We need to forge a path toward a world where the dynamics of past hurts and emotional wounds are no longer tolerated, where empathy and compassion triumph over cruelty and the power of defeat. We can stand as beacons of understanding, unwavering in our commitment to unravel the complexities and create a brighter future by reclaiming the power of resiliency—the inner power to rise above our thoughts, feelings and emotions.

In order to break the cycle of past hurts our imperfection from the negative impact, it is crucial to develop a deep understanding of its patterns and dynamics. Recognizing these patterns is the first step towards interrupting the cycle and preventing its continuation. It is coming to terms with the fact that if a glass of mike falls and breaks, there is no need to cry over spilled milk. We need to work on preventing it from spilling. We reclaim power by not allowing our feelings to control our emotions.

Imagine growing up in a household where verbal and emotional abuse were a daily occurrence. We may have witnessed our parents engaging in aggressive arguments and seen the damaging effects of their words on each other. As we enter adulthood, we may find ourselves replicating the same patterns we witnessed in our relationships. The cycle seems inescapable, and we can feel trapped.

However, by reclaiming the power of creating a healthy neuropathway, we can embrace the imperfection we experienced as a child and not allow it to determine how we live. If we repeat what we witness, we are not tapping into the power within us. Attending a support group or finding professional support may assist in finding our true selves. This realization can ignite a spark within us—a desire to understand the dynamics of our negative past and put an end to the destructive patterns that have plagued our lives for so long.

We all need to embark on self-reflection and education. We need to find resources, books, and professional guidance to gain a comprehensive understanding of the cycle of past negative thoughts. Through our newfound knowledge, we may begin to identify the warning signs and red flags of past hurts. We may recognize the insidious ways that manipulation, control, and power imbalances play out in our relationships and interactions with others. Armed with this understanding, we may feel empowered to interrupt the cycle and prevent its continuation. This is an indicator of reclaiming power.

We have to summon the courage to confront the toxic patterns that have been absorbed from the past. We must understand that breaking the cycle requires setting firm boundaries and refusing to tolerate any form of hurt, whether subtle or overt. This meant no longer accepting demeaning comments, controlling behaviours, or any action undermining our worth and autonomy.

As we start implementing these changes, we will face resistance from those who seek to maintain the status quo. Some people in our lives may be unwilling to relinquish our power and control. However, we must persist, seeking support from our newfound network of survivors and advocates who believe in reclaiming the power.

Over time, we will begin to witness the transformative effects of breaking the cycle of imperfect thoughts, emotions and feelings. We will discover our innate resilience and strength as we nurture our emotional well-being and rebuild our self-esteem. With each step forward, we may distance ourselves from the pain of our past and embrace a future where our imperfections become our friends.

Our story can be a testament to the power of recognizing and interrupting the cycle of imperfection. By understanding its dynamics and bravely taking action, we can liberate ourselves from the chains of past hurts and set a new course for our lives—one defined by empowerment, healthy relationships, and personal growth.

Learning to embrace our imperfections is possible; by working together with survivours, you can create a ripple effect of change, fostering a world where our past has no room to thrive. We can reclaim the power taken from us due to past hurts.

As survivors of a negative past, healing emotional wounds is an essential part of our journey toward reclaiming our well-being and rebuilding our self-esteem. The impact of our negative past can run deep, leaving scars that can be visible and hidden within the depths of our souls. Yet, through resilience and a commitment to our healing, we can embark on a path of emotional recovery as we reclaim the power of freedom.

The journey begins with acknowledging the negative thoughts, emotions and feelings that stem from our past. It takes courage to confront the emotions buried beneath the surface, but it is a necessary step toward healing and embracing the hurts. By allowing ourselves to experience and express our emotions fully, we create space for healing and release reclaiming power.

Nurturing our emotional well-being involves creating a safe and supportive environment. This may mean seeking help to recondition our minds and restructure our thoughts. Surrounding ourselves with people who understand and believe in our healing journey can be transformative; we are energized by others who are supportive and have reclaimed their power.

Rebuilding self-esteem requires a shift in perspective. We must challenge the negative beliefs that have been ingrained within us. We can learn to treat ourselves with kindness and gentleness through self-compassion and self-care, embracing the "who" we are. Engaging in activities that bring us joy and a sense of accomplishment helps to rebuild our sense of worth and confidence.

Healing emotional wounds involves setting boundaries to protect ourselves from further harm. Learning to say no to toxic relationships and situations empowers us to prioritize what is most important. We can reclaim our autonomy by asserting our boundaries and creating a space where healing can flourish. We can come to terms with forgiving ourselves and others who may have wronged us. The power to be who we see ourselves to be can become a reality as we embrace our past.

It's important to remember that healing is not linear. It is a process that unfolds at its own pace, with ups and downs along the way. Some days may be more challenging than others, but each step forward, no matter how small, brings us closer to reclaiming our emotional well-being.

As we continue our healing journey, let us be gentle with ourselves and celebrate our progress. We are not defined by our past experiences but rather by our resilience and the strength we embody as we strive to heal our emotional wounds. Together, we can nurture our well-being and rebuild our self-esteem, creating a future filled with healing, hope, and happiness.

It is a profound and empowering process of reclaiming power after experiencing a negative past that left emotional scars. It begins with a deep longing for autonomy and the desire to regain control over our lives and choices. In the aftermath, the sense of self can be shattered, and the survivor may feel trapped, powerless, and stripped of their independence. However, within the depths of their being lies an unyielding spirit yearning to break free from the chains of the past. That's the unreclaimed power.

PERSONAL POWER

Personal power is a transformative endeavour that requires self-exploration, courage, and a willingness to confront the wounds inflicted by the past. It starts with acknowledging the pain and trauma endured and finding the strength to embark on a healing journey. As we embark on this path, we can recognize that our experiences do not define us but rather serve as stepping stones toward reclaiming our power. We can embrace our imperfections as we see value in them and how we can be empowered from our negative past.

One crucial aspect of personal power is reconnecting with one's voice and intuition. It involves peeling away the layers of self-doubt and fear ingrained from the past, embracing the validity of our thoughts, feelings, and emotions, and steering them in a healthy pathway. We can then trust ourselves again and recognize that our perspective is valuable and deserves to be honoured.

We must learn how to set healthy boundaries internally and in our relationships. Boundaries become a shield of protection, allowing us to prioritize our needs, preferences, and well-being. Saying "no" becomes an act of self-care and self-respect, as we recognize our right to make choices that align with our values and aspirations.

Personal power involves embracing vulnerability. It means allowing ourselves to be open to new experiences, relationships, and possibilities, even in the face of past pain. It requires the willingness to take risks, knowing that setbacks and challenges may arise along the way. With each step forward, we build resilience and cultivate a profound sense of empowerment, knowing that we have the capacity to shape our own destiny.

As we rediscover our power, we can become the authors of our lives, free from the constraints of our past. It is not without its difficulties, but it is marked by moments of profound growth, self-discovery, and renewed hope. Through our courage and determination, we can emerge as warriors, reclaiming our autonomy and embracing a future filled with limitless possibilities.

One crucial aspect of rediscovering personal power is that our sense of self-worth and identity can be deeply shaken. The activities and interests that once brought us joy and a sense of empowerment may have been overshadowed or forgotten entirely. Rediscovering personal power involves embarking on a process of self-exploration and reconnecting with the activities and interests that ignite a spark within us. We need to dig into the depths of our being and listen to the whispers of our true selves, even if we have been suppressed or silenced for a long time.

We need to create a safe and nurturing space for ourselves. This may involve seeking support from trusted individuals who can provide encouragement and understanding. It may require creating boundaries and setting aside dedicated time for personal exploration without judgment or interruption.

As we get back on track with this path, we may find ourselves drawn to activities and interests we used to enjoy or always wanted to explore. It could be reconnecting with an artistic pursuit, such as painting, writing, or playing a musical instrument. It might involve engaging in physical activities that bring a sense of vitality and strength, including dancing, yoga, or hiking in nature.

PERSONAL POWER

RECONNECTING *with* OURSELVES

Reconnecting with ourselves is about engaging in these activities and embracing the emotions they evoke within us. It is about allowing ourselves to fully immerse in the present moment and rediscover the joy, fulfilment, and sense of purpose they bring. It may take time and patience as we navigate through any emotional barriers or fears that may arise, but with each step forward, we are reclaiming a part of ourselves that was once lost.

As we reconnect with ourselves, we may begin to witness the transformative power they hold. They become vehicles for self-expression, outlets for emotions, and sources of inspiration. They may remind us of our inherent strengths and ignite a renewed sense of empowerment. Engaging in these activities not only nourishes our souls but also serves as a reminder that we are deserving of happiness and fulfilment.

Through reconnecting with ourselves, we reclaim a vital part of ourselves that our negative past may have tried to diminish, creating a feeling of imperfection. We can embrace our unique interests and talents, and in doing so, we cultivate a deeper understanding of who we are and what brings us genuine happiness. It is a journey of self-discovery growth, and a testament to our resilience.

As we continue on this path, we may find that our power evolves and changes and that is perfectly natural. The critical aspect is the process of exploration, the willingness to be open to new experiences, and the courage to embrace what truly brings us joy and empowers us.

It is in reconnecting with ourselves that we reclaim our authentic selves. And, in doing so, we pave the way for a life filled with purpose, fulfilment, and a renewed sense of personal strength. We need to be survivour of our past by reclaiming ourselves and recognizing that each essential step towards our future can bring healing and rebuilding to our lives. It can signify a journey of rediscovering our inner strength and regaining control over our lives and decision-making processes. The path to reconnecting with ourselves may seem daunting, but by following these empowering steps, we can embark on a transformative journey of self-empowerment and growth.

It is essential to acknowledge the impact of our past on our lives. By recognizing that our negative past is not our fault, we can begin to let go of any misplaced guilt or self-blame. We make wrong decisions and mistakes based on a cause. We may experience abuse traumas and grow up in a toxic family that is responsible for emotional scars. This acknowledgement lays the foundation for reclaiming ourselves and reclaiming control over our lives.

Developing self-awareness is a crucial component. It involves taking the time for introspection and reflection, allowing us to understand our desires, needs, and boundaries. By reconnecting with our true selves, separate from the influence of our past, we can start rebuilding a solid foundation for regaining ourselves.

Setting boundaries can become a fundamental aspect of

reclaiming who we are. We must clearly define what is acceptable and unacceptable in our interactions with others. This requires courage and the willingness to communicate and uphold these boundaries. We create a safe space for ourselves by establishing and enforcing healthy boundaries.

Reconnecting with ourselves is not an overnight process. It is a series of small steps that we take toward regaining control over our lives. Starting with manageable tasks and gradually expanding our comfort zones is important. Each milestone should be celebrated, no matter how small, as it reinforces our sense of agency and reminds us of our progress.

Making decisions is a significant aspect of regaining ourselves. We can start by making choices in simple day-to-day matters and gradually progress to more significant life decisions. Each decision reinforces our ability to shape our lives and strengthens our sense of empowerment.

Reconnecting with ourselves often involves personal growth and self-discovery. Engaging in activities that promote personal development, such as therapy, self-help books, or pursuing new interests, allows us to expand our horizons and regain a sense of purpose. This growth journey is an opportunity to rediscover ourselves and nurture our personal growth.

Throughout this process, it is essential to embrace imperfection. Setbacks may occur, and it's important to show ourselves compassion and understanding. Self-forgiveness and patience are imperative elements of regaining control over our lives. Reconnecting with ourselves allows us to learn from our experiences and continue moving forward on our path toward autonomy.

Celebrating moments of independence and self-reliance is an empowering practice. Whether it's achieving a personal goal, making a decision without seeking validation, or asserting our boundaries, these moments remind us of our growing autonomy and reinforce our belief in our ability to shape our lives.

Cultivating self-trust is deeply intertwined with reconnecting ourselves. Learning to trust our instincts, judgments, and decisions allows us to rely on ourselves and have confidence in our ability to navigate life's challenges. Developing self-trust empowers us to make choices aligned with our values and desires, ultimately leading to a greater sense of autonomy.

Reconnecting with ourselves after a negative past is a profound and transformative journey. It requires strength, perseverance, and a steadfast belief in our worth. By acknowledging the impact of our past, building inner awareness, setting boundaries, seeking support, taking small steps, making decisions, embracing personal growth imperfections, celebrating independence, and cultivating self-trust, we can gradually take back our lives.

One of the most empowering steps we can take for emotional healing is through the pursuit of education. We can learn to embrace imperfection by not doubting ourselves and knowing what we can and cannot do. We need to be accurate and honest with ourselves about our limitations. Education can become a beacon of light, guiding us toward a path of healing, growth, and self-empowerment.

Acquiring knowledge after experiencing an unhealthy past is not just about gaining information; it is about arming ourselves with the tools and resources to make informed choices. It is a transformative process that expands our understanding of ourselves, our rights, and the world around us.

Through education, we can begin to unravel the complexities of our negative past, understanding its dynamics and recognizing the patterns that once held us captive. We can explore the psychological, emotional, and social aspects of our negative past, and gaining insights into the tactics employed and how they impact our lives is important.

Education becomes a lens through which we view our past experiences with newfound clarity, replacing confusion with comprehension.

The power of knowledge should be a catalyst for change. We can learn about the resources available to help catapult our future. We can explore support groups, counselling services, and legal protections. Education empowers us to confidently navigate these systems and seek the assistance we need to heal and rebuild.

Furthermore, education ignites our curiosity and opens doors to new possibilities. We can explore topics that resonate with our personal experiences, diving into psychology, trauma recovery, self-care, and empowerment. We can engage in self-reflection, uncovering our strengths, values, and aspirations. We can discover our inherent worth and recognize that we have the capacity to create a life filled with joy, purpose, and fulfilment.

Education can give us the language to articulate our experiences, allowing us to share our stories with others on a similar journey. Through education, we can find our voice, advocate for ourselves and raise awareness about the issues surrounding our negative past. We can become part of a broader community, connecting with others, experts, and advocates who offer support, guidance, and encouragement.

As we acquire knowledge and gain a deeper understanding of ourselves, we can cultivate a sense of empowerment that transcends the boundaries of our past. Education can become the stepping stone towards reclaiming our personal power, enabling us to make choices that align with our values, aspirations, and well-being.

By reconnecting with ourselves, we can transform victimhood into survivorship. It's a profound shift that involves moving away from a victim mentality and embracing the strength, resilience, and inner resources that lie within.

Imagine enduring the devastating impact of the past, feeling trapped in the shadows of our past, and carrying the weight of our unhealthy experiences, wrong choices or mistakes. Regrets can make us see ourselves as a victim. Our suffering and powerlessness should not define us to change our circumstances, as the power is in our hands. Deep within our hearts, a flicker of hope still burns—a spark waiting to ignite the transformation.

You need to acknowledge and recognize the power of perception. While you may have been a victim of your past, it doesn't define your entire being. You are more than the pain you've endured. You can rewrite your narrative by shifting your mindset and embracing your innate strength.

With each small step forward, you can see glimpses of your resilience. You can find the courage to confront your past, unravelling the layers of trauma that have bound you. It's not easy, but you can refuse to let your past define your future.

Support becomes your anchor—a lifeline that guides you through the process. You can seek out trusted individuals, therapists, support groups, or friends who can offer a safe space for healing and growth. Together, you work towards unravelling the emotional wounds inflicted by past abuse, traumas, past mistakes, wrong decisions and regrets, gently nurturing your wounded spirit back to life.

As you progress, you will begin to rediscover your personal power. You can reclaim your autonomy, understanding that you have control over your choices, actions, and boundaries. Through therapy, self-reflection, and self-care practices, you can cultivate a deep sense of self-compassion—a gentle reminder that you deserve love, kindness, and understanding.

You can engage in empowering activities that bring joy and a renewed sense of purpose. It may be exploring creative outlets, reconnecting with forgotten passions, or engaging in physical activities that strengthen your body, soul and spirit. These experiences can become catalysts for your transformation, allowing you to redefine your identity and embrace your newfound strength.

You may stumble upon setbacks and triggers, but you will persevere, armed with resilience and an unwavering determination to heal. You can develop coping strategies and learn to lean on your support network during difficult times. You may realize that healing is not a linear process but a winding path where growth emerges from every twist and turn.

As you emerge from the shadows of victimhood, you may step into the light of your empowerment. You can become a beacon of hope for others still trapped in the darkness, inspiring them to find their strength and reminding them that they, too, can reclaim their power.

Transforming victimhood into survivorship is a journey of self-discovery, resilience, and healing. But with each step forward, you can embrace your true essence—an embodiment of courage, resilience, and unwavering determination to live a life free from the shackles of our past hurts.

In the face of adversity, there lies a remarkable opportunity for transformation and personal growth. Abuse, traumas, past mistakes, wrong decisions and regrets are painful and unjust experiences that can be harnessed as a catalyst for profound change and empowerment. By embracing our transformative potential, we can embark on a journey of healing, resilience, and self-discovery.

When we begin the process of transforming into growth, it is essential to acknowledge the strength and courage it takes to confront our past experiences. This acknowledgment serves as a foundation for our journey, empowering us to reclaim our inner power and rewrite our narrative.

We need to cultivate a positive mindset and extend understanding towards ourselves. Recognizing that our past cannot change allows us to release self-blame or guilt, freeing us from the shackles of victimhood. Through self-compassion, we open the door to self-love and acceptance, nurturing our wounded inner selves with kindness and patience.

As we explore our healing, we can discover the lessons hidden within our experiences. Every adversity carries valuable insights that can shape our perspectives and strengthen our resilience. By examining the impact of our past abuse, traumas, mistakes, wrong decisions and regrets on our lives, we gain wisdom and learn to make empowering choices. We embrace the belief that our past does not define us but our ability to rise above it.

Harnessing the transformative potential involves redefining our identity. We no longer see ourselves solely as victims but as survivors with a remarkable capacity for growth and change. With this shift in mindset, we can tap into our inherent resilience, recognizing that we have the power to create a life of purpose and fulfilment.

As we progress along our path, we can seek out resources and support systems that can aid in our transformation. Whether it be therapy, support groups, or trusted confidants, surrounding ourselves with individuals who understand and validate our experiences can be immensely healing. Through these connections, we gain strength, encouragement, and a sense of belonging that further propels our growth.

Amidst the process of transforming our negative past into growth, it is crucial to celebrate our victories, no matter how small. Each step forward is a testament to our resilience and determination. By acknowledging and honouring our progress, we reinforce our belief in our ability to overcome adversity and create a brighter future.

Ultimately, transforming into growth is an empowering journey that requires commitment, self-compassion, and an unwavering belief in our potential. By embracing the transformative power within us, we heal our wounds and pave the way for others to embark on their journeys of healing and growth.

As we rise above the pain, we can become beacons of inspiration and hope, living testaments to the incredible strength of the human spirit. We can reclaim our power, voice, and right to a life filled with love, joy, and limitless possibilities. Together, we rewrite our stories, transforming the darkness into a tapestry of resilience, growth, and empowerment.

As a survivor, you will have endured immense pain and faced countless challenges. The scars of your past may have left you feeling broken and lost, but within you lies an incredible strength waiting to be awakened. It is time to reclaim your power and embark on a journey of healing, transformation, and, ultimately, thriving.

Thriving is not just about surviving; it is about rediscovering your worth, reclaiming your identity, and embracing your limitless potential. It also requires you to nurture a sense of self-compassion to acknowledge the incredible resilience that has carried you through the darkest times.

To thrive is to cultivate a fulfilling and meaningful life beyond the impact of abuse, traumas, past mistakes, wrong decisions and regrets. It means embracing the truth that you are not defined by your past but rather by your choices in the present moment. It is about reclaiming your personal power and recognizing that you have the ability to shape your destiny.

Thriving is not an easy path. It requires courage, vulnerability, and a willingness to face your deepest wounds. It calls for you to confront the lingering shadows of fear and insecurity that may still haunt you. Yet, within this journey lies the opportunity for profound growth and transformation.

As you embark on the path of thriving, you must surround yourself with a supportive network of individuals who uplift and empower you. You will need to create a safe space to openly share your experiences, triumphs, and setbacks. You can lean on one another for guidance, encouragement, and understanding.

Thriving also involves rediscovering your passions and interests, those activities that bring you joy and ignite your soul. It is through reconnecting with these aspects of yourself that you find a sense of purpose and fulfilment. Whether engaging in creative pursuits, exploring nature, or pursuing educational opportunities, you can use these avenues to reclaim your autonomy and rebuild your life.

The journey of thriving is not without its challenges. You may stumble and face setbacks along the way. However, each obstacle you overcome serves as a testament to your strength and resilience. You learn to celebrate your progress, no matter how small, and to be patient and gentle with yourself during moments of self-doubt.

Ultimately, thriving is a lifelong commitment to your well-being and growth. It is a testament to the indomitable spirit within us, refusing to be defined by our past but instead embracing the infinite possibilities of our future. Through healing, self-discovery, and the cultivation of resilience, you can rise above the pain and create a life that is not only free from the shackles of abuse, traumas, past mistakes, wrong decisions and regrets but filled with joy, purpose, and an unwavering sense of self-worth.

As we reach the end of this chapter on reclaiming power and recovery, we reflect upon the incredible strength and resilience within each survivor. Throughout this transformative journey, we have delved deep into the dynamics of the issues of life, gaining insights into its patterns and effects. We have embarked on a path of healing, nurturing our emotional well-being, and rebuilding our self-esteem.

Breaking the cycle has been a powerful step on our journey. We have recognized the importance of interrupting the patterns of abuse, traumas, past mistakes, wrong decisions, and regrets to prevent their continuation, not only for ourselves but for future generations. Through our healing process, we have reclaimed our personal agency, rediscovering and asserting our autonomy and ability to make choices.

In our pursuit of reclaiming power, we have reconnected with our personal passions. We have rediscovered activities and interests that bring us joy and a profound sense of empowerment. Engaging in these pursuits has strengthened our sense of self and regained a deeper connection to our personal identity.

Reclaiming autonomy has been a significant milestone on our journey. We have regained control over our lives and decision-making processes, refusing to let our past define us. We have embraced education and empowerment, acquiring knowledge and resources to make informed choices and navigate our path toward a brighter future.

Through our resilience and determination, we have transformed from victims to survivors. We have shifted our mindset, embracing the strength and courage that resides within us. Our experiences from the past have not defined us but have become catalysts for growth and personal empowerment.

As we conclude this chapter, we do so with a sense of hope and possibility. We have learned to harness the transformative potential of our experiences, using them as fuel for personal growth and empowerment. We have cultivated resilience and embraced the belief that we can thrive beyond the impact of our negative past.

Your past does not define you. You are a survivor, a testament to your strength and resilience. As you continue on this journey of healing and reclaiming power, may you remember the profound depths of your inner strength. Embrace the possibilities that lie ahead, knowing that you have the capacity to create a life of fulfilment and meaning.

May you continue to cultivate resilience and personal growth. Thrive beyond the impact of the negative past, knowing that you are worthy of love, happiness, and a life filled with empowerment. Your story is one of strength, and as you reclaim your power, may your light shine brightly, inspiring others on their paths of healing and recovery.

EMBRACE
IMPERFECTIONS

In the journey of life, we all encounter challenges and go through unpredicted issues that can affect us in the long term. They can make us feel imperfect, leaving us broken. We often find ourselves stumbling upon the rocky terrain of abuse, traumas, addictions, toxic relationships and a negative past, wrong decisions, mistakes, and regrets, creating emotional wounds and brokenness. However, we need to *"Embrace Imperfections."* We've all been there, feeling the weight of our imperfections and the nagging voice in our heads that whispers, "You're not good enough." But what if we could rewrite that narrative? What if we could embrace our imperfections as stepping stones towards growth and self-discovery? We must embark on a transformative exploration of the power within our mistakes with an understanding of *"Embrace Imperfections."* This means challenging societal expectations, shattering the illusion of perfection, and embracing the beauty of being human.

Navigating the treacherous waters of failure and setbacks, armed with the knowledge that holds invaluable lessons, can help us see our missteps not as reflections of our worth but as opportunities for growth and self-improvement.

We need to peel back the layers of regret, freeing ourselves from the shackles of past choices and missed opportunities. We have to capture the art of self-acceptance, discovering the liberating truth that our worthiness is not contingent upon flawlessness. It is in our imperfections that we find our true strength. This is the power of resilience of understanding how to *"Embrace Imperfections."* from emotional wounds.

We can learn from our missteps, cultivate a growth mindset, and celebrate the beauty of progress, no matter how small. We can rewrite a story from the weight of regret or the fear of failure. We must embrace imperfection, unlocking the immense potential within our flawed yet extraordinary selves. Let's embark on this transformative quest and discover the boundless possibilities that await us on the other side of embracing imperfections.

Have you ever found yourself held back by the paralyzing fear of failure? That nagging voice in your head that tells you to play it safe, avoid risks, and stay within your comfort zone? It's an everyday struggle that many of us face on our journey toward personal growth and self-discovery. But let me share with you a transformative perspective that can liberate you from the grip of this fear and open doors to a world of possibilities.

We must recognize that mistakes are not the enemy. In fact, they are our most outstanding teachers. Every stumble and misstep holds valuable lessons that can guide us toward a brighter future. So, let go of the notion that mistakes are a reflection of your worth or competence. They are simply stepping stones on the growth path.

Imagine a world where failure is seen not as a final destination but as a necessary part of the journey. Embrace the idea that failure is not an indication of your worth but an opportunity for learning, growth, and resilience. By shifting your perspective, you free yourself from the suffocating fear that holds you back. Embrace the belief that failure is not the end of the road but a detour leading you to new insights and unforeseen possibilities.

Every successful person you admire has encountered failure along their path. They've stumbled, fallen, and faced setbacks. But what sets them apart is their unwavering determination to persevere, learn from their mistakes, and keep moving forward. They understand that failure is not a defining moment but a stepping stone toward success.

Embracing growth means letting go of perfectionism. It means accepting that you are a work in progress, constantly evolving and learning. Permit yourself to take risks, knowing that you'll gain wisdom and experience even if you stumble. Allow yourself to embrace vulnerability, for it is through vulnerability that proper growth and connection thrive.

Failure is not the end of the road but a necessary part of the journey. Each setback brings you closer to the person you are meant to become. So, be kind to yourself when you make mistakes. Celebrate the lessons they offer and use them as fuel to propel you forward.

As you navigate the intricate tapestry of life, know that you discover your true strength and resilience in the face of failure. Embrace imperfection, for it is through our flaws that our unique beauty shines. Embrace growth, for it is in the pursuit of growth that we find fulfillment and purpose.

With each step you take toward overcoming the fear of failure, you unlock a world of possibilities and open yourself up to a life that is rich with meaning and growth. Embrace the journey, and let your mistakes become the stepping stones that guide you toward your brightest future.

In a world that constantly bombards us with messages of

perfection, it's easy to fall into the trap of believing that we must meet impossible standards to be worthy and lovable. But this is further from the truth. Embracing imperfections is not a sign of weakness or failure; it's a testament to our shared humanity. We are all beautifully flawed beings navigating through life's unpredictable journey. It's in these imperfections that we find our true strength and authenticity.

Society may try to convince us that perfection is the ultimate goal, but embracing imperfections means embracing growth, vulnerability, and self-discovery. It means acknowledging that life is a constant work in progress, and that's okay.

When we accept ourselves as we are, we create space for personal growth and self-compassion. We release the heavy burden of self-judgment and allow ourselves to experience genuine joy and fulfillment. It's a radical act of self-love that empowers us to live authentically, embracing both our strengths and weaknesses.

We connect with others on a deeper level through our imperfections. Our vulnerabilities become bridges that lead to compassion and understanding. We inspire others to do the same when we share our stories, struggles, and triumphs. We create a community of acceptance and support where everyone feels valued and understood.

Let go of the need for perfection. Embrace the beauty of your imperfections. Embrace the growth that comes from making mistakes and learning from them. Embrace the unique journey that is yours and yours alone. You are deserving of love, respect, and kindness precisely as you are. Embrace yourself wholeheartedly, and let your imperfections shine. They are the very things that make you beautifully human.

Mistakes, we all make them; they are the imperfections we have. They're an inevitable part of being human. But those very mistakes hold incredible potential for growth and personal development. Within the depths of our errors lie invaluable lessons that can shape us into wiser, more resilient individuals.

As you stumble upon a rocky path, you make a misstep that makes you tumble. It's painful embarrassing, and you find yourself questioning your judgment. But here's the thing - when you pick yourself up and dust off the dirt, you realize that the fall has left you with newfound knowledge and insight. In these moments of vulnerability, we discover our capacity to learn from our mistakes.

Learning from mistakes isn't about dwelling on the past or beating ourselves up over what went wrong. It's about acknowledging our missteps with a curious and open mind, knowing that we can *"Embrace Imperfections."* It's about embracing the opportunity to dissect our choices, actions, and consequences to glean valuable lessons. It's about understanding we have value and worth and that the brokenness can be beneficial in understanding how to prevent future hurt and support those who are hurt.

How do we extract those lessons? It starts with self-reflection. Take a moment to pause and delve into the heart of your mistakes. What were the factors that led to them? What blind spots or assumptions were you operating under? By unravelling the layers, you'll uncover patterns and insights to guide you toward personal growth.

Learning from mistakes is also about taking ownership of them. Accept responsibility for your actions instead of deflecting blame or wallowing in regret. This doesn't mean berating yourself endlessly but rather recognizing that your choices played a role in the outcome. By owning your mistakes, you empower yourself to make different choices in the future.

We need to use our mistakes to fuel personal development. Armed with newfound wisdom, we have the opportunity to make conscious, intentional changes in our lives. Perhaps you realize the importance of setting boundaries or trusting your instincts more. Maybe you uncover a deeper understanding of your values or discover the significance of self-care. Personal growth is a continuous journey. Learning from mistakes is an ongoing process that requires patience, self-compassion, and a willingness to adapt. Each mistake is a stepping stone towards a better version of yourself that is more resilient, insightful, and capable of making choices aligned with your values and aspirations.

We must learn to embrace imperfection, knowing we can still be progressive. Embrace the mistakes that have sculpted your path. They are not to be discarded or forgotten but rather cherished as the catalysts for your personal development. Extract those valuable lessons, internalize them, and let them guide you toward a future brimming with growth, fulfillment, and the wisdom that can only come from learning from your mistakes.

In the depths of our hearts, regrets can linger like heavy chains, weighing us down with what-ifs and what-could-have-been. We find ourselves trapped in the clutches of the past, constantly replaying moments that went awry, endlessly berating ourselves for the choices we wish we could undo.

Life is a masterful symphony of experiences, and every note, whether harmonious or dissonant, contributes to the grand composition of our existence. In the face of regret, we discover the immense power of letting go and embracing the infinite possibilities of second chances.

Picture yourself standing on the precipice of a vast, sun-kissed horizon. The warm breeze whispers gently, coaxing you to release the grip on those regrets that have held you captive for far too long. In this moment, in the gentle caress of the wind, you begin to understand the transformative journey ahead.

To let go of regret is not to dismiss or forget the past but rather to release its hold on your present and future. It is an act of courage, a declaration that you refuse to be defined by yesterday's missteps. With each step forward, you shed the weight of remorse, allowing yourself the freedom to move, grow, and blossom.

Embracing second chances is a dance with the unknown, a

symphony of possibility. It is the recognition that life's path is not linear but a winding, meandering road brimming with unexpected twists and turns. As you let go of regret, you open yourself to the serendipitous encounters and unforeseen opportunities that await you on this remarkable journey.

Take a moment to envision a canvas stretched before you, awaiting the vibrant strokes of your reinvention. With each brushstroke, you paint a new narrative woven with resilience, self-compassion, and an unwavering belief in the beauty of your imperfect self. Even if you feel broken, you can still implement your colours, creating a priceless piece of art. Through the lens of acceptance and growth, you begin to see regret not as a burden but as a catalyst for profound transformation.

Embrace the freedom that comes with letting go. Release the regrets that have held you captive and step into the realm of possibility. With each choice you make, with each breath you take, remember that you are the author of your own story—a story of resilience, redemption, and the audacious pursuit of a future brimming with happiness and fulfillment. Embrace the journey of embracing second chances, for it is in this embrace that you will find the boundless magic of a life lived with open arms.

In a world driven by materialistic pursuits and external validation, it's all too easy to fall into the trap of measuring success solely by external achievements. We are bombarded with messages that equate success with wealth, status, and accolades, leaving little room for introspection and personal fulfillment. But what if there's more to success than meets the eye? What if true success lies in a more profound, more meaningful realm?

Redefining success begins with a shift in perspective. It's about breaking free from societal expectations and re-evaluating what truly matters to us as individuals. It's an invitation to embark on a journey of self-discovery and self-reflection, where we explore the values and passions that resonate with our souls.

True success encompasses various aspects of our lives. It goes beyond mere financial wealth and professional accomplishments. It embraces our emotional well-being, relationships, personal growth, and contributions to the world.

As we embark on the path of redefining success, we start by turning inward. We take the time to question our values and priorities. We ask ourselves, "What brings me joy? What ignites my passion? What impact do I want to have in the world?" These introspective inquiries serve as guideposts to navigate the uncharted territory of a more holistic definition of success.

Even in brokenness, we can still progress in our destiny. We still carry value and worth and can be beneficial to those in our world. Our brokenness does not determine our future.

We need to value personal growth and self-actualization. We understand that success lies in reaching the destination and the transformative process we undergo along the way. We embrace the challenges and setbacks as opportunities for growth, recognizing that resilience and perseverance are as important as any external accolades.

Relationships take center stage as we redefine success. We recognize the significance of deep connections, love, and support. We prioritize nurturing meaningful relationships and creating a positive impact on the lives of others. Success becomes intertwined with our ability to foster empathy, compassion, and kindness towards ourselves and those around us.

Redefining success also involves aligning our actions with our values. We cultivate a sense of purpose and live in alignment with our authentic selves. We let go of societal expectations and embrace our unique paths, even if they deviate from the mainstream notions of success. It's about finding fulfillment in pursuing our passions, making a difference in our communities, and living a life that is true to who we are.

In this paradigm shift, we can discover that success is not a fixed destination but an ever-evolving journey. It is a continuous process of self-discovery, growth, and contribution. As we expand our definition of success, we find joy and contentment in the small victories and everyday moments that make life meaningful.

In a world that often celebrates strength and perfection, the concept of vulnerability can seem unsettling. We are conditioned to hide our flaws, shield our insecurities, and present a polished facade to the world. However, true growth and connection can only be achieved when we embrace vulnerability, allowing ourselves to be seen authentically as imperfections.

Emily is a woman who has spent most of her life meticulously crafting an image of perfection. She believed that vulnerability was a weakness and that showing her true self would expose her to judgment. As a result, she built walls around her heart, never letting anyone get too close.

One day, Emily found herself at a crossroads. She realized that her pursuit of perfection had left her feeling isolated and disconnected from others. She yearned for genuine connections and a sense of belonging. At this pivotal moment, she decided to embark on a journey of embracing vulnerability. Emily began by reflecting on her fears and insecurities. She acknowledged that vulnerability required her to let go of the illusion of control and open herself up to the possibility of rejection and judgment. It was a daunting prospect, but she knew that a genuine connection could only be forged when she allowed herself to be seen authentically. She did not allow herself to become useless but valuable.

Emily learned that embracing her imperfections was a powerful act of self-acceptance. She recognized that her flaws and vulnerabilities were not weaknesses but unique aspects of her humanity. Instead of hiding them, she started to view them as opportunities for growth and connection.

Emily's journey took her to places she never thought she would go. She found the courage to share her insecurities with trusted friends and loved ones, opening up conversations beyond surface-level interactions. In doing so, she discovered that vulnerability begets vulnerability, and by sharing her authentic self, she invited others to do the same.

As Emily continued to embrace vulnerability, she noticed a profound shift in her relationships. She created an environment of trust and authenticity by allowing herself to be seen authentically. Others felt safe to open up to her, and together, they formed deep and meaningful connections based on genuine understanding and acceptance.

Emily realized that vulnerability was not a one-time act but an ongoing practice. She learned to celebrate her growth and acknowledge the progress she made along the way. It wasn't always easy, and there were moments of discomfort, but the rewards of authentic connection far outweighed the fear of judgment.

Emily's journey of embracing vulnerability taught her that true strength lies in the ability to be vulnerable and authentic. By shedding the armour of perfection, she found a profound sense of belonging and a deeper connection with herself and others. As she continued on her path, she discovered the beauty in imperfections and the transformative power of vulnerability.

In a world that often glorifies perfection and achievements, embracing imperfections can be a transformative journey toward personal growth and fulfillment. Cultivating a growth mindset is about shifting our perspective and emphasizing progress and learning rather than fixating on flawless outcomes.

A positive mindset acknowledges that challenges and setbacks are essential parts of life. It recognizes that failure is not a reflection of our worth or abilities but rather an opportunity for growth. Instead of being discouraged by mistakes, those with a growth mindset see them as stepping stones on the path to improvement.

To develop a positive mindset, reframing how we perceive failure and setbacks is crucial. Rather than viewing them as permanent obstacles, we can see them as temporary setbacks that provide valuable lessons. This mindset allows us to approach challenges with resilience and a willingness to learn from our experiences.

We need to see that we can change our future regardless of our flaws, weaknesses, wrongdoings, wrong choices, and mistakes in life. Our past does not determine our future. Therefore, let's *"Embrace Imperfections,"* knowing that we don't have to live in the past. Embracing a positive mindset involves valuing effort and perseverance. Instead of seeking immediate perfection, we focus on our progress through consistent practice and dedication. We understand mastery takes time and that each small step forward is significant.

A positive mindset is rooted in curiosity and a hunger for knowledge. It encourages us to embrace new learning opportunities and to seek out feedback as a means of improvement. We become open to different perspectives, ideas, and constructive criticism, recognizing that they can help refine our skills and expand our horizons.

Moreover, developing a positive mindset requires self-compassion. We learn to treat ourselves with kindness and understanding when we make mistakes or face challenges. We approach ourselves with empathy and encouragement rather than engaging in self-criticism or negative self-talk. This self-compassion enables us to bounce back from setbacks and maintain a positive attitude towards growth.

In practicing a positive mindset, we create an environment that fosters learning and personal development. We can become more adaptable, resilient, and open to change. Challenges become opportunities, and setbacks become springboards for progress. We embrace the journey of self-improvement, understanding that it is not about reaching an unattainable standard of perfection but rather about continuously evolving and expanding our capabilities.

By cultivating a positive mindset, we unlock our potential and tap into the power of continuous growth. We free ourselves from the burden of unattainable perfection and embrace the beauty of our imperfections. In doing so, we embark on a fulfilling and meaningful journey of self-discovery, progress, and lifelong learning.

We often measure our success based on significant accomplishments, overlooking the significance of small steps and incremental progress. However, actual growth lies in embracing imperfections and recognizing the value of every small win.

Life is a series of moments; within each moment, there are opportunities for growth and learning. Celebrating small wins is about shifting our focus from the end goal to the process. It's about acknowledging the effort, perseverance, and resilience we demonstrate as we navigate the challenges that come our way.

When we celebrate small wins, we cultivate a positive mindset and build self-confidence. No matter how seemingly insignificant, each small victory contributes to our overall progress. Whether completing a task, taking a step out of our comfort zone, or making a positive change in our habits, these small wins deserve to be acknowledged and celebrated.

Recognizing and appreciating our progress reinforces a sense of accomplishment and motivation. It fuels our determination to keep moving forward despite setbacks or obstacles. Small wins provide us with momentum and encouragement, reminding us that growth is a continuous journey composed of many small steps.

Moreover, celebrating small wins allows us to find joy in the present moment, observing that in the midst of our brokenness, we can still be an asset to something or somebody. It helps us cultivate gratitude and an appreciation for the effort we invest in ourselves. Rather than solely focusing on the destination, we learn to relish the journey itself, savouring the little victories that shape our path.

To *"Embrace Imperfections"* means embracing the idea that progress is not always linear. It's about understanding that setbacks and mistakes are inevitable, but they don't define our worth or invalidate our progress. By celebrating small wins, we shift our mindset towards growth and self-compassion. We learn to recognize that even in the face of imperfections, we continuously evolve and become better versions of ourselves.

Let us embrace the beauty of small wins. Let us appreciate the power of progress, no matter how incremental. Each step forward, no matter how small, brings us closer to our goals and aspirations. Celebrating these moments is a testament to our resilience, determination, and unwavering commitment to personal growth. Remember, the journey itself, composed of countless small wins, makes life truly fulfilling and meaningful.

Life is a constant journey of change. It is marked by the ebb and flow of positive and negative experiences. Within this ever-shifting landscape, embracing change and adapting is crucial for personal growth and fulfillment. Learning to welcome new challenges and opportunities can be transformative in a world that often values perfection and consistency.

Change can be intimidating. It disrupts our comfort zones and forces us to confront the unknown. Yet, it is through change that we discover new possibilities and unlock hidden potential within ourselves. Embracing change means acknowledging that life is a dynamic process and growth often happens outside of our comfort zones.

Adaptability is the key to thriving amidst change. It involves being open to new perspectives, ideas, and ways of doing things. Instead of resisting or fearing change, we learn to navigate it with resilience and flexibility. We understand that change is an invitation for growth and self-discovery.

By welcoming new challenges, we invite opportunities for personal development. Each challenge presents a chance to test our skills, expand our knowledge, and uncover hidden strengths. Embracing these challenges allows us to step outside the boundaries of what we thought was possible, paving the way for transformative growth.

Growth opportunities often come disguised as setbacks or failures. When we approach them with an open mind and a willingness to learn, they become stepping stones towards personal and professional advancement. Embracing these opportunities means embracing the lessons they offer, even if they come packaged in moments of discomfort or uncertainty.

Embracing change and adaptability requires a mindset shift. It means letting go of rigid expectations and embracing the beauty of imperfection, knowing that even if we are broken, we still have value. Rather than striving for an unattainable notion of perfection, we learn to appreciate the growth that comes from embracing our flaws and shortcomings. We understand that our greatest strengths often emerge from our vulnerabilities.

We need to embrace change and adaptability. Together, we will navigate the ever-changing currents of life, discovering our true potential and finding fulfillment in the beautiful imperfections that make us who we are.

We have embarked on a transformative journey of embracing imperfection recognizing the immense power and beauty that lies within our flaws and mistakes. We have challenged the fear of failure, understanding that mistakes are not setbacks but stepping stones for growth and self-improvement.

Central to our journey has been the embrace of self-acceptance, acknowledging that imperfection is an intrinsic part of the human experience. We have learned to let go of regret, releasing ourselves from the burdens of the past and instead focusing on the present and the endless possibilities.

As we have explored the concept of success, we have broadened our definition, moving beyond external achievements and embracing a more holistic perspective. We understand that true success is found in personal growth, meaningful connections, and living in alignment with our values.

Embracing vulnerability has been an empowering aspect of our journey. We have allowed ourselves to be seen authentically, embracing our imperfections with courage and openness. Through this vulnerability, we have formed deeper connections with ourselves and others, creating spaces of genuine understanding and acceptance.

A growth mindset has become our compass, guiding us towards progress and learning rather than fixating on perfection. We have cultivated self-compassion, extended kindness and understanding of ourselves when things go wrong. Through this practice, we have learned to celebrate small wins, recognizing and appreciating the progress we make, no matter how small.

As we conclude this chapter, we do so with a renewed sense of optimism and empowerment. We have learned to embrace change and adaptability, welcoming new challenges and opportunities for growth with open arms. We understand that life is a continuous journey of learning and evolving, and it is in our imperfections that we find the beauty and potential for transformation.

This is a reminder that you are a magnificent work in progress. Embrace your imperfections, for they are the brushstrokes that make your unique and beautiful canvas. Embrace the journey of growth and self-discovery, knowing that every mistake and setback is an opportunity for learning and becoming a better version of yourself.

May you continue to walk this path with resilience, compassion, and a deep appreciation for the imperfect beauty that resides within you.

Embrace the extraordinary power of imperfection, and may it guide you toward a life filled with authenticity, growth, and fulfillment.

EMBRACE
IMPERFECTIONS

In the journey of life, we all encounter challenges and go through unpredicted issues that can affect us in the long term. They can make us feel imperfect, leaving us broken. We often find ourselves stumbling upon the rocky terrain of abuse, traumas, addictions, toxic relationships and a negative past, wrong decisions, mistakes, and regrets, creating emotional wounds and brokenness. However, we need to *"Embrace Imperfections."* We've all been there, feeling the weight of our imperfections and the nagging voice in our heads that whispers, "You're not good enough." But what if we could rewrite that narrative? What if we could embrace our imperfections as stepping stones towards growth and self-discovery? We must embark on a transformative exploration of the power within our mistakes with an understanding of *"Embrace Imperfections."* This means challenging societal expectations, shattering the illusion of perfection, and embracing the beauty of being human.

Navigating the treacherous waters of failure and setbacks, armed with the knowledge that holds invaluable lessons, can help us see our missteps not as reflections of our worth but as opportunities for growth and self-improvement.

We need to peel back the layers of regret, freeing ourselves from the shackles of past choices and missed opportunities. We have to capture the art of self-acceptance, discovering the liberating truth that our worthiness is not contingent upon flawlessness. It is in our imperfections that we find our true strength. This is the power of resilience of understanding how to *"Embrace Imperfections."* from emotional wounds.

We can learn from our missteps, cultivate a growth mindset, and celebrate the beauty of progress, no matter how small. We can rewrite a story from the weight of regret or the fear of failure. We must embrace imperfection, unlocking the immense potential within our flawed yet extraordinary selves. Let's embark on this transformative quest and discover the boundless possibilities that await us on the other side of embracing imperfections.

Have you ever found yourself held back by the paralyzing fear of failure? That nagging voice in your head that tells you to play it safe, avoid risks, and stay within your comfort zone? It's an everyday struggle that many of us face on our journey toward personal growth and self-discovery. But let me share with you a transformative perspective that can liberate you from the grip of this fear and open doors to a world of possibilities.

We must recognize that mistakes are not the enemy. In fact, they are our most outstanding teachers. Every stumble and misstep holds valuable lessons that can guide us toward a brighter future. So, let go of the notion that mistakes are a reflection of your worth or competence. They are simply stepping stones on the growth path.

Imagine a world where failure is seen not as a final destination but as a necessary part of the journey. Embrace the idea that failure is not an indication of your worth but an opportunity for learning, growth, and resilience. By shifting your perspective, you free yourself from the suffocating fear that holds you back. Embrace the belief that failure is not the end of the road but a detour leading you to new insights and unforeseen possibilities.

Every successful person you admire has encountered failure along their path. They've stumbled, fallen, and faced setbacks. But what sets them apart is their unwavering determination to persevere, learn from their mistakes, and keep moving forward. They understand that failure is not a defining moment but a stepping stone toward success.

Embracing growth means letting go of perfectionism. It means accepting that you are a work in progress, constantly evolving and learning. Permit yourself to take risks, knowing that you'll gain wisdom and experience even if you stumble. Allow yourself to embrace vulnerability, for it is through vulnerability that proper growth and connection thrive.

Failure is not the end of the road but a necessary part of the journey. Each setback brings you closer to the person you are meant to become. So, be kind to yourself when you make mistakes. Celebrate the lessons they offer and use them as fuel to propel you forward.

As you navigate the intricate tapestry of life, know that you discover your true strength and resilience in the face of failure. Embrace imperfection, for it is through our flaws that our unique beauty shines. Embrace growth, for it is in the pursuit of growth that we find fulfillment and purpose.

With each step you take toward overcoming the fear of failure, you unlock a world of possibilities and open yourself up to a life that is rich with meaning and growth. Embrace the journey, and let your mistakes become the stepping stones that guide you toward your brightest future.

In a world that constantly bombards us with messages of

perfection, it's easy to fall into the trap of believing that we must meet impossible standards to be worthy and lovable. But this is further from the truth. Embracing imperfections is not a sign of weakness or failure; it's a testament to our shared humanity. We are all beautifully flawed beings navigating through life's unpredictable journey. It's in these imperfections that we find our true strength and authenticity.

Society may try to convince us that perfection is the ultimate goal, but embracing imperfections means embracing growth, vulnerability, and self-discovery. It means acknowledging that life is a constant work in progress, and that's okay.

When we accept ourselves as we are, we create space for personal growth and self-compassion. We release the heavy burden of self-judgment and allow ourselves to experience genuine joy and fulfillment. It's a radical act of self-love that empowers us to live authentically, embracing both our strengths and weaknesses.

We connect with others on a deeper level through our imperfections. Our vulnerabilities become bridges that lead to compassion and understanding. We inspire others to do the same when we share our stories, struggles, and triumphs. We create a community of acceptance and support where everyone feels valued and understood.

Let go of the need for perfection. Embrace the beauty of your imperfections. Embrace the growth that comes from making mistakes and learning from them. Embrace the unique journey that is yours and yours alone. You are deserving of love, respect, and kindness precisely as you are. Embrace yourself wholeheartedly, and let your imperfections shine. They are the very things that make you beautifully human.

Mistakes, we all make them; they are the imperfections we have. They're an inevitable part of being human. But those very mistakes hold incredible potential for growth and personal development. Within the depths of our errors lie invaluable lessons that can shape us into wiser, more resilient individuals.

As you stumble upon a rocky path, you make a misstep that makes you tumble. It's painful embarrassing, and you find yourself questioning your judgment. But here's the thing - when you pick yourself up and dust off the dirt, you realize that the fall has left you with newfound knowledge and insight. In these moments of vulnerability, we discover our capacity to learn from our mistakes.

Learning from mistakes isn't about dwelling on the past or beating ourselves up over what went wrong. It's about acknowledging our missteps with a curious and open mind, knowing that we can *"Embrace Imperfections."* It's about embracing the opportunity to dissect our choices, actions, and consequences to glean valuable lessons. It's about understanding we have value and worth and that the brokenness can be beneficial in understanding how to prevent future hurt and support those who are hurt.

How do we extract those lessons? It starts with self-reflection. Take a moment to pause and delve into the heart of your mistakes. What were the factors that led to them? What blind spots or assumptions were you operating under? By unravelling the layers, you'll uncover patterns and insights to guide you toward personal growth.

Learning from mistakes is also about taking ownership of them. Accept responsibility for your actions instead of deflecting blame or wallowing in regret. This doesn't mean berating yourself endlessly but rather recognizing that your choices played a role in the outcome. By owning your mistakes, you empower yourself to make different choices in the future.

We need to use our mistakes to fuel personal development. Armed with newfound wisdom, we have the opportunity to make conscious, intentional changes in our lives. Perhaps you realize the importance of setting boundaries or trusting your instincts more. Maybe you uncover a deeper understanding of your values or discover the significance of self-care. Personal growth is a continuous journey. Learning from mistakes is an ongoing process that requires patience,

51 | P a g e

self-compassion, and a willingness to adapt. Each mistake is a stepping stone towards a better version of yourself that is more resilient, insightful, and capable of making choices aligned with your values and aspirations.

We must learn to embrace imperfection, knowing we can still be progressive. Embrace the mistakes that have sculpted your path. They are not to be discarded or forgotten but rather cherished as the catalysts for your personal development. Extract those valuable lessons, internalize them, and let them guide you toward a future brimming with growth, fulfillment, and the wisdom that can only come from learning from your mistakes.

In the depths of our hearts, regrets can linger like heavy chains, weighing us down with what-ifs and what-could-have-been. We find ourselves trapped in the clutches of the past, constantly replaying moments that went awry, endlessly berating ourselves for the choices we wish we could undo.

Life is a masterful symphony of experiences, and every note, whether harmonious or dissonant, contributes to the grand composition of our existence. In the face of regret, we discover the immense power of letting go and embracing the infinite possibilities of second chances.

Picture yourself standing on the precipice of a vast, sun-kissed horizon. The warm breeze whispers gently, coaxing you to release the grip on those regrets that have held you captive for far too long. In this moment, in the gentle caress of the wind, you begin to understand the transformative journey ahead.

To let go of regret is not to dismiss or forget the past but rather to release its hold on your present and future. It is an act of courage, a declaration that you refuse to be defined by yesterday's missteps. With each step forward, you shed the weight of remorse, allowing yourself the freedom to move, grow, and blossom.

Embracing second chances is a dance with the unknown, a

symphony of possibility. It is the recognition that life's path is not linear but a winding, meandering road brimming with unexpected twists and turns. As you let go of regret, you open yourself to the serendipitous encounters and unforeseen opportunities that await you on this remarkable journey.

Take a moment to envision a canvas stretched before you, awaiting the vibrant strokes of your reinvention. With each brushstroke, you paint a new narrative woven with resilience, self-compassion, and an unwavering belief in the beauty of your imperfect self. Even if you feel broken, you can still implement your colours, creating a priceless piece of art. Through the lens of acceptance and growth, you begin to see regret not as a burden but as a catalyst for profound transformation.

Embrace the freedom that comes with letting go. Release the regrets that have held you captive and step into the realm of possibility. With each choice you make, with each breath you take, remember that you are the author of your own story—a story of resilience, redemption, and the audacious pursuit of a future brimming with happiness and fulfillment. Embrace the journey of embracing second chances, for it is in this embrace that you will find the boundless magic of a life lived with open arms.

In a world driven by materialistic pursuits and external validation, it's all too easy to fall into the trap of measuring success solely by external achievements. We are bombarded with messages that equate success with wealth, status, and accolades, leaving little room for introspection and personal fulfillment. But what if there's more to success than meets the eye? What if true success lies in a more profound, more meaningful realm?

Redefining success begins with a shift in perspective. It's about breaking free from societal expectations and re-evaluating what truly matters to us as individuals. It's an invitation to embark on a journey of self-discovery and self-reflection, where we explore the values and passions that resonate with our souls.

True success encompasses various aspects of our lives. It goes beyond mere financial wealth and professional accomplishments. It embraces our emotional well-being, relationships, personal growth, and contributions to the world.

As we embark on the path of redefining success, we start by turning inward. We take the time to question our values and priorities. We ask ourselves, "What brings me joy? What ignites my passion? What impact do I want to have in the world?" These introspective inquiries serve as guideposts to navigate the uncharted territory of a more holistic definition of success.

Even in brokenness, we can still progress in our destiny. We still carry value and worth and can be beneficial to those in our world. Our brokenness does not determine our future.

We need to value personal growth and self-actualization. We understand that success lies in reaching the destination and the transformative process we undergo along the way. We embrace the challenges and setbacks as opportunities for growth, recognizing that resilience and perseverance are as important as any external accolades.

Relationships take center stage as we redefine success. We recognize the significance of deep connections, love, and support. We prioritize nurturing meaningful relationships and creating a positive impact on the lives of others. Success becomes intertwined with our ability to foster empathy, compassion, and kindness towards ourselves and those around us.

Redefining success also involves aligning our actions with our values. We cultivate a sense of purpose and live in alignment with our authentic selves. We let go of societal expectations and embrace our unique paths, even if they deviate from the mainstream notions of success. It's about finding fulfillment in pursuing our passions, making a difference in our communities, and living a life that is true to who we are.

In this paradigm shift, we can discover that success is not a fixed destination but an ever-evolving journey. It is a continuous process of self-discovery, growth, and contribution. As we expand our definition of success, we find joy and contentment in the small victories and everyday moments that make life meaningful.

In a world that often celebrates strength and perfection, the concept of vulnerability can seem unsettling. We are conditioned to hide our flaws, shield our insecurities, and present a polished facade to the world. However, true growth and connection can only be achieved when we embrace vulnerability, allowing ourselves to be seen authentically as imperfections.

Emily is a woman who has spent most of her life meticulously crafting an image of perfection. She believed that vulnerability was a weakness and that showing her true self would expose her to judgment. As a result, she built walls around her heart, never letting anyone get too close.

One day, Emily found herself at a crossroads. She realized that her pursuit of perfection had left her feeling isolated and disconnected from others. She yearned for genuine connections and a sense of belonging. At this pivotal moment, she decided to embark on a journey of embracing vulnerability. Emily began by reflecting on her fears and insecurities. She acknowledged that vulnerability required her to let go of the illusion of control and open herself up to the possibility of rejection and judgment. It was a daunting prospect, but she knew that a genuine connection could only be forged when she allowed herself to be seen authentically. She did not allow herself to become useless but valuable.

Emily learned that embracing her imperfections was a powerful act of self-acceptance. She recognized that her flaws and vulnerabilities were not weaknesses but unique aspects of her humanity. Instead of hiding them, she started to view them as opportunities for growth and connection.

Emily's journey took her to places she never thought she would go. She found the courage to share her insecurities with trusted friends and loved ones, opening up conversations beyond surface-level interactions. In doing so, she discovered that vulnerability begets vulnerability, and by sharing her authentic self, she invited others to do the same.

As Emily continued to embrace vulnerability, she noticed a profound shift in her relationships. She created an environment of trust and authenticity by allowing herself to be seen authentically. Others felt safe to open up to her, and together, they formed deep and meaningful connections based on genuine understanding and acceptance.

Emily realized that vulnerability was not a one-time act but an ongoing practice. She learned to celebrate her growth and acknowledge the progress she made along the way. It wasn't always easy, and there were moments of discomfort, but the rewards of authentic connection far outweighed the fear of judgment.

Emily's journey of embracing vulnerability taught her that true strength lies in the ability to be vulnerable and authentic. By shedding the armour of perfection, she found a profound sense of belonging and a deeper connection with herself and others. As she continued on her path, she discovered the beauty in imperfections and the transformative power of vulnerability.

In a world that often glorifies perfection and achievements, embracing imperfections can be a transformative journey toward personal growth and fulfillment. Cultivating a growth mindset is about shifting our perspective and emphasizing progress and learning rather than fixating on flawless outcomes.

A positive mindset acknowledges that challenges and setbacks are essential parts of life. It recognizes that failure is not a reflection of our worth or abilities but rather an opportunity for growth. Instead of being discouraged by mistakes, those with a growth mindset see them as stepping stones on the path to improvement.

To develop a positive mindset, reframing how we perceive failure and setbacks is crucial. Rather than viewing them as permanent obstacles, we can see them as temporary setbacks that provide valuable lessons. This mindset allows us to approach challenges with resilience and a willingness to learn from our experiences.

We need to see that we can change our future regardless of our flaws, weaknesses, wrongdoings, wrong choices, and mistakes in life. Our past does not determine our future. Therefore, let's *"Embrace Imperfections,"* knowing that we don't have to live in the past. Embracing a positive mindset involves valuing effort and perseverance. Instead of seeking immediate perfection, we focus on our progress through consistent practice and dedication. We understand mastery takes time and that each small step forward is significant.

A positive mindset is rooted in curiosity and a hunger for knowledge. It encourages us to embrace new learning opportunities and to seek out feedback as a means of improvement. We become open to different perspectives, ideas, and constructive criticism, recognizing that they can help refine our skills and expand our horizons.

Moreover, developing a positive mindset requires self-compassion. We learn to treat ourselves with kindness and understanding when we make mistakes or face challenges. We approach ourselves with empathy and encouragement rather than engaging in self-criticism or negative self-talk. This self-compassion enables us to bounce back from setbacks and maintain a positive attitude towards growth.

In practicing a positive mindset, we create an environment that fosters learning and personal development. We can become more adaptable, resilient, and open to change. Challenges become opportunities, and setbacks become springboards for progress. We embrace the journey of self-improvement, understanding that it is not about reaching an unattainable standard of perfection but rather about continuously evolving and expanding our capabilities.

By cultivating a positive mindset, we unlock our potential and tap into the power of continuous growth. We free ourselves from the burden of unattainable perfection and embrace the beauty of our imperfections. In doing so, we embark on a fulfilling and meaningful journey of self-discovery, progress, and lifelong learning.

We often measure our success based on significant accomplishments, overlooking the significance of small steps and incremental progress. However, actual growth lies in embracing imperfections and recognizing the value of every small win.

Life is a series of moments; within each moment, there are opportunities for growth and learning. Celebrating small wins is about shifting our focus from the end goal to the process. It's about acknowledging the effort, perseverance, and resilience we demonstrate as we navigate the challenges that come our way.

When we celebrate small wins, we cultivate a positive mindset and build self-confidence. No matter how seemingly insignificant, each small victory contributes to our overall progress. Whether completing a task, taking a step out of our comfort zone, or making a positive change in our habits, these small wins deserve to be acknowledged and celebrated.

Recognizing and appreciating our progress reinforces a sense of accomplishment and motivation. It fuels our determination to keep moving forward despite setbacks or obstacles. Small wins provide us with momentum and encouragement, reminding us that growth is a continuous journey composed of many small steps.

Moreover, celebrating small wins allows us to find joy in the present moment, observing that in the midst of our brokenness, we can still be an asset to something or somebody. It helps us cultivate gratitude and an appreciation for the effort we invest in ourselves. Rather than solely focusing on the destination, we learn to relish the journey itself, savouring the little victories that shape our path.

To *"Embrace Imperfections"* means embracing the idea that progress is not always linear. It's about understanding that setbacks and mistakes are inevitable, but they don't define our worth or invalidate our progress. By celebrating small wins, we shift our mindset towards growth and self-compassion. We learn to recognize that even in the face of imperfections, we continuously evolve and become better versions of ourselves.

Let us embrace the beauty of small wins. Let us appreciate the power of progress, no matter how incremental. Each step forward, no matter how small, brings us closer to our goals and aspirations. Celebrating these moments is a testament to our resilience, determination, and unwavering commitment to personal growth. Remember, the journey itself, composed of countless small wins, makes life truly fulfilling and meaningful.

Life is a constant journey of change. It is marked by the ebb and flow of positive and negative experiences. Within this ever-shifting landscape, embracing change and adapting is crucial for personal growth and fulfillment. Learning to welcome new challenges and opportunities can be transformative in a world that often values perfection and consistency.

Change can be intimidating. It disrupts our comfort zones and forces us to confront the unknown. Yet, it is through change that we discover new possibilities and unlock hidden potential within ourselves. Embracing change means acknowledging that life is a dynamic process and growth often happens outside of our comfort zones.

Adaptability is the key to thriving amidst change. It involves being open to new perspectives, ideas, and ways of doing things. Instead of resisting or fearing change, we learn to navigate it with resilience and flexibility. We understand that change is an invitation for growth and self-discovery.

By welcoming new challenges, we invite opportunities for personal development. Each challenge presents a chance to test our skills, expand our knowledge, and uncover hidden strengths. Embracing these challenges allows us to step outside the boundaries of what we thought was possible, paving the way for transformative growth.

Growth opportunities often come disguised as setbacks or failures. When we approach them with an open mind and a willingness to learn, they become stepping stones towards personal and professional advancement. Embracing these opportunities means embracing the lessons they offer, even if they come packaged in moments of discomfort or uncertainty.

Embracing change and adaptability requires a mindset shift. It means letting go of rigid expectations and embracing the beauty of imperfection, knowing that even if we are broken, we still have value. Rather than striving for an unattainable notion of perfection, we learn to appreciate the growth that comes from embracing our flaws and shortcomings. We understand that our greatest strengths often emerge from our vulnerabilities.

We need to embrace change and adaptability. Together, we will navigate the ever-changing currents of life, discovering our true potential and finding fulfillment in the beautiful imperfections that make us who we are.

We have embarked on a transformative journey of embracing imperfection recognizing the immense power and beauty that lies within our flaws and mistakes. We have challenged the fear of failure, understanding that mistakes are not setbacks but stepping stones for growth and self-improvement.

Central to our journey has been the embrace of self-acceptance, acknowledging that imperfection is an intrinsic part of the human experience. We have learned to let go of regret, releasing ourselves from the burdens of the past and instead focusing on the present and the endless possibilities.

As we have explored the concept of success, we have broadened our definition, moving beyond external achievements and embracing a more holistic perspective. We understand that true success is found in personal growth, meaningful connections, and living in alignment with our values.

Embracing vulnerability has been an empowering aspect of our journey. We have allowed ourselves to be seen authentically, embracing our imperfections with courage and openness. Through this vulnerability, we have formed deeper connections with ourselves and others, creating spaces of genuine understanding and acceptance.

A growth mindset has become our compass, guiding us towards progress and learning rather than fixating on perfection. We have cultivated self-compassion, extended kindness and understanding of ourselves when things go wrong. Through this practice, we have learned to celebrate small wins, recognizing and appreciating the progress we make, no matter how small.

As we conclude this chapter, we do so with a renewed sense of optimism and empowerment. We have learned to embrace change and adaptability, welcoming new challenges and opportunities for growth with open arms. We understand that life is a continuous journey of learning and evolving, and it is in our imperfections that we find the beauty and potential for transformation.

This is a reminder that you are a magnificent work in progress. Embrace your imperfections, for they are the brushstrokes that make your unique and beautiful canvas. Embrace the journey of growth and self-discovery, knowing that every mistake and setback is an opportunity for learning and becoming a better version of yourself.

May you continue to walk this path with resilience, compassion, and a deep appreciation for the imperfect beauty that resides within you.

EMBRACE IMPERFECTIONS

Embrace the extraordinary power of imperfection, and may it guide you toward a life filled with authenticity, growth, and fulfillment.

MEANING *and* PURPOSE

After enduring the harrowing journey of a negative past, it's natural to question the meaning and purpose of it all. The aftermath can leave us feeling lost, disconnected, and unsure of our place in the world. However, within the depths of our pain lies an opportunity for profound self-discovery and growth.

Discovering meaning and purpose is a transformative process that requires introspection and a willingness to explore the depths of our being. It starts with acknowledging that our experiences, although difficult, have shaped us into who we are today. We can recognize that our past does not define us but rather serves as a catalyst for our personal evolution. We acknowledge that we are not perfect; we all carry flaws and weaknesses, and even when broken, we still hold value and worth. We need to remind ourselves to *"Embrace Imperfections."*

In the midst of healing, we may embark on a journey to seek meaning—a quest to understand the more profound significance of our experiences. This exploration involves peering into the core of our values, beliefs, and aspirations. Some may ask ourselves: "What truly matters to me?" "What are the principles that guide my life?" "What do I yearn to contribute to the world?" We still want to contribute even if we are broken and emotionally wounded. We are like crayons; even though we may be broken, we can still draw. This gives meaning and purpose. We can see the value to *"Embrace Imperfections."*

As we delve into these profound questions, we may uncover a renewed sense of purpose. Our issues become a powerful catalyst for personal growth, propelling us to make a difference in the lives of others who have experienced similar hardships. Through our pain, we become advocates, allies, and sources of inspiration for those still on their healing journeys.

Discovering meaning and purpose involves reconnecting with our authentic selves. Life's challenges have a way of fracturing our sense of identity, but we can mend the broken pieces through introspection and self-reflection. We explore our passions, talents, and interests, reclaiming the parts of ourselves that were overshadowed by our negative experiences.

In this process of finding meaning and purpose, we may stumble upon unexpected gifts and strengths. We realize that our resilience and courage in the face of adversity have shaped us into remarkable individuals. Our issues can become the fuel that ignites our determination to live a life aligned with our true selves.

Discovering meaning and purpose, we may encounter obstacles and moments of doubt. However, it is through these challenges that our true strength and resilience shine. With each step forward, we will begin to create a life that is deeply meaningful and purposeful—a life that honours our experiences embraces our values, and empowers us to make a positive impact.

Within life's challenges lies a profound opportunity for meaning and purpose. It is a journey in which we can navigate the complexities of healing, with the ultimate goal of becoming more assertive, wiser, and more resilient.

Meaning and purpose is a concept that transcends mere survival. It invites us to embrace the challenges we have faced as catalysts for profound personal change. It is not a quick fix or a linear path but a courageous and introspective exploration of one's inner landscape.

Through the process of healing, we can come to understand the tremendous strength and resilience we possess. We can recognize the impact challenges have had on our lives and the potential to find meaning and purpose within us. This transformative shift in perspective allows us to view our experiences as opportunities for learning, self-discovery, and profound personal evolution.

As we progress on our healing journey, we can notice subtle shifts in our thoughts, emotions, and outlook on life. We can understand the perspectives to *"Embrace Imperfections."* We will develop a renewed appreciation for the simple joys and moments of connection. We will savour the present, understanding that we have emerged from the darkness and can now fully embrace the light.

Meaning and purpose involve deepening empathy and compassion for oneself and others who have experienced similar journeys. We can learn to hold space for our pain and find solace in connecting with others who understand and validate our experiences. We can form a resilient community bound by our shared strength and determination.

In the midst of meaning and purpose, we can re-evaluate our priorities and values. We can gain clarity on what truly matters to us and make intentional choices aligned with our newfound understanding. We may pursue passions we once believed were unattainable or become advocates for change, using our experiences to bring about positive transformations in our own lives and the lives of others.

The path of meaning and purpose is not without challenges.

There will be setbacks, moments of doubt, and days when the weight of the past feels overwhelming. However, through these very struggles, we can discover our resilience and courage. We can rise above adversity, find strength in vulnerability and continue to move forward despite obstacles.

Meaning and purpose are a testament to the indomitable human spirit. It is a narrative of hope, resilience, and the enduring power of the human soul to overcome even the most devastating experiences. It serves as a reminder that healing is possible and can lead to profound personal transformation.

Within the realm of meaning and purpose, intricate layers are waiting to be unravelled, offering us practical guidance and coping strategies to aid us in our journey of healing and transformation. It is a landscape adorned with resilience, courage, and the unyielding human spirit.

As we embark on our path of meaning and purpose, we may encounter a myriad of challenges and emotions. It is a process that requires gentle self-exploration, patience, and a willingness to face the remnants of our past. As we focus on the depths of our issues, we will peel back layers of pain and vulnerability while holding onto the flicker of hope that lies within.

Guidance on this transformative journey is multifaceted. It begins with recognizing that healing is not a linear process but a nonlinear dance between progress and setbacks. We will learn to embrace the ebb and flow of our emotions, allowing ourselves to grieve, feel anger, and find solace in moments of peace.

Coping strategies become our trusted companions, offering support and stability in the face of adversity. Mindfulness and grounding techniques provide anchors in times of distress, helping survivors navigate the overwhelming waves of emotion. Through these practices, we can learn to reconnect with the present moment, anchoring ourselves in the here and now.

Self-care rituals become a sacred act of self-nurturing as we discover the power of caring for our physical, emotional, and mental well-being. We create personalized practices that replenish our energy, whether it be through gentle exercise, journaling, or immersing ourselves in nature's embrace. These rituals become beacons of self-compassion, reminding ourselves that we deserve love and care.

The support of others is vital in the journey of meaning and purpose. We seek connections with individuals who can hold space for our experiences, providing a safe haven where we can share our stories without judgment. We may engage in support group therapy sessions or cultivate relationships with loved ones who offer unwavering support and understanding.

As we progress, we cultivate a newfound sense of purpose and meaning. We seek opportunities for personal meaning and purpose, transforming our issues into a catalyst for positive change. This may involve engaging in advocacy work, sharing our experiences to raise awareness, or finding solace in creative outlets that allow us to express ourselves authentically.

The intricacies of meaning and purpose lie in the delicate balance between self-reflection and forward movement. We can learn to honour our past while embracing the possibilities of our future. We can navigate the complexities of forgiveness for ourselves and those who have caused us harm. We redefine our identity, no longer defined solely by our challenges but by the strength, resilience, and wisdom we have cultivated along our journey. Ultimately, meaning and purpose offer us an opportunity to survive and thrive.

Picture yourself on this journey, navigating the twists and turns of self-improvement. As you strive to shed old habits, there will be moments of triumph and moments of struggle. It's easy to get caught up in the overwhelming nature of the ultimate goal, losing sight of the significance of each small step forward. But remember, progress is not always measured by giant leaps but by the accumulation of consistent efforts.

Celebrate the moments when you resist the pull of old habits, those instances when you consciously choose a healthier path. It could be the first time you resist the temptation to reach for that sugary snack or the day you complete a workout, even when your motivation is waning. These seemingly insignificant moments are stepping stones towards lasting change and deserve recognition.

Take a pause and reflect on how far you've come. Look back at the person you were when you first embarked on this journey and compare it to who you are now. Celebrate the meaning, purpose, resilience, and determination that have carried you to this point. Acknowledge the inner strength you've cultivated and the positive choices you've made along the way. Celebrate the person you are becoming.

It's also essential to find joy in the small victories. Break down your ultimate goal into smaller milestones achievable in the shorter term. When you reach these milestones, no matter how modest they may be, take a moment to revel in your accomplishment. Treat yourself to something special—a small indulgence, a moment of relaxation, or a joyful activity that brings you happiness. These celebrations serve as reminders of your progress and fuel your motivation to keep going.

Remember that setbacks are a natural part of any journey. When you encounter obstacles or slip back into old habits, be compassionate with yourself. Instead of dwelling on perceived failures, focus on the lessons learned and the resilience gained from those experiences. Embrace setbacks as opportunities, meaning and purpose and celebrate the strength it takes to get back on track.

Share your milestones with those who support and uplift you. Let your loved ones in on your achievements, whether big or small.

Their encouragement and celebration amplify your joy and validate the significance of your progress. Find solace in the community, whether it's a close friend, a support group, or an online community. Connect with others who understand your challenges and can offer support and cheer you on during each milestone.

In this journey towards shedding bad habits and regaining the strength from self-destructive behaviours, celebrating milestones becomes a crucial chapter—an ode to the progress made and a testament to your commitment to finding meaning and purpose. Recognize the significance of each small step forward, rejoice in the moments of triumph, and cultivate a mindset of positivity and self-appreciation. With each milestone celebrated, you strengthen your resolve and reinforce the belief that you are capable of creating lasting change.

As the winds of change carry you forward on your journey of shedding self-destructive behaviours, there comes a crucial point where sustaining positive change becomes the focus. It is at this juncture that you lay the foundation for long-term success, establishing strategies and practices that will safeguard the progress you have made and propel you toward a brighter, healthier future.

Imagine yourself at this pivotal moment, standing on the precipice of a transformed life. The habits you once clung to, which held you back, have gradually given way to healthier choices and new behaviour patterns. But how do you ensure this newfound progress endures, becoming an intrinsic part of your identity rather than a fleeting change?

Sustaining positive change begins with a deep-rooted commitment to yourself. Recognize the significance of your progress and reaffirm your dedication to a healthier and more fulfilling life. Embrace the belief that you can maintain this positive trajectory and deserve the happiness and well-being that come with it.

Develop strategies that will support your long-term success.

Reflect on the practices and routines that have helped you shed your self-destructive habits thus far. Identify the triggers and temptations that can pull you back into old patterns and devise strategies to mitigate their influence. This could involve creating a supportive environment, surrounding yourself with positive influences, and establishing boundaries to protect your progress.

Establish healthy habits as a solid framework for sustained positive change. Consistency is vital, as it solidifies new behaviours and minimizes the likelihood of slipping back into old patterns. Integrate these habits into your daily routine, making them a non-negotiable part of your life. Whether it's dedicating time to exercise, preparing nutritious meals, practicing mindfulness, or seeking moments of self-care, commit to these habits wholeheartedly.

Find joy in the journey. Sustaining positive change is not just about maintaining discipline; it's about embracing the beauty of the process itself. Celebrate the small victories, relish in the progress you continue to make, and savour the moments of meaning, purpose and self-discovery along the way. Cultivate gratitude for the opportunity to transform your life and let it fuel your determination to stay the course.

Embrace a meaning and purpose mindset, as discussed earlier that views challenges as opportunities for learning and growth. Recognize that setbacks are a natural part of any journey and see them as stepping stones rather than roadblocks. When faced with obstacles, assess them objectively, extract the lessons they hold, and use them to further refine your strategies for sustaining positive change.

Above all, be kind and patient with yourself. Recognize that sustaining positive change is a lifelong commitment, and there may be times when you stumble or falter. Embrace these moments as opportunities on your journey to find meaning and purpose. Learn to forgive yourself, recalibrate, and recommit to your journey. Remember that every day is a fresh start—a chance to reaffirm your dedication and continue the legacy of positive change you have begun.

POSITIVE MINDSET

The power of a positive mindset is undeniable. It shapes our perceptions, influences our emotions, and fuels our actions. When we embrace positivity, we open ourselves to a world of possibilities, where obstacles become opportunities and setbacks transform into stepping stones towards personal growth and success. However, maintaining a positive mindset requires conscious effort and a commitment to self-improvement.

We must explore the science behind conditioning the mind for positivity, understanding how our thoughts and beliefs can be rewired to create a more optimistic outlook on life. We need to explore practical techniques and strategies that can help us challenge and reframe negative thoughts, develop gratitude as a daily practice, and embrace failure as an essential part of the journey toward success.

Additionally, we must explore the significance of positive self-talk; discovering how we speak to ourselves can shape our reality. By cultivating a supportive and encouraging inner dialogue, we can uplift our spirits, boost our confidence, and foster a deep sense of self-belief.

Finding joy in the present moment is a crucial aspect we need to explore. Often, our minds wander between regrets of the past and anxieties about the future, causing us to miss the beauty and opportunities available right now. By practicing mindfulness and embracing the present, we can cultivate a greater appreciation for life's small pleasures and experiences.

Furthermore, we need to explore the importance of engaging in activities that bring us genuine happiness and fulfillment. Nurturing our passions and prioritizing self-care rejuvenates our spirits and strengthens our overall well-being. Also, the power of forgiveness and letting go, understanding how releasing past resentments can free us from emotional burdens and enable us to move forward with a lighter heart.

Embracing optimism as a way of life must be a central theme to reduce stress and anxiety and allow the past to float away from our present. It's the key to *"Embrace Imperfections"* from abuse, traumas, addictions, toxic relationships, a negative past, regrets, mistakes, and wrong doing.

Adopting an optimistic mindset can positively impact our lives, relationships, and overall happiness. By shifting our perspective and focusing on the possibilities and potential inherent in every situation, we can create a life infused with hope, resilience, and a deep appreciation for the journey.

Sustaining a positive mindset requires consistent practice. We need practical tips and strategies to incorporate into our daily routines, ensuring positivity becomes a habit rather than a fleeting state of mind. By nurturing our minds and conditioning ourselves to stay positive, we can lay the foundation for a lifetime of happiness and fulfillment.

A positive mindset is a powerful tool that can significantly impact our lives and world experience. It is the foundation upon which we build our thoughts, emotions, and actions, shaping our perceptions and influencing our overall well-being. Understanding the power of a positive mindset requires recognizing its profound effects on various aspects of our lives. It will enable us to approach challenges and obstacles with resilience and optimism. Instead of being overwhelmed by difficulties, we will view them as opportunities for growth and learning. It is our ability to find solutions and persevere that increases our chances of overcoming obstacles and achieving success.

Moreover, a positive mindset enhances our emotional well-being. When we adopt a positive outlook, we tend to experience more positive emotions, such as joy, gratitude, and contentment. These positive emotions have a ripple effect, influencing our overall mood and improving our mental and emotional state. By focusing on the positive aspects of our lives, we can counteract negative emotions and cultivate a sense of well-being.

A positive mindset enhances our relationships and social interactions. When we approach others with positivity, we radiate warmth and kindness, creating a positive environment that fosters more profound connections. Our positive attitude attracts like-minded individuals and strengthens existing relationships. By maintaining an optimistic perspective, we can build and nurture meaningful connections that enrich our lives.

Furthermore, a positive mindset can improve our physical health. It can positively impact our immune system, cardiovascular health, and overall well-being. When we maintain a positive mindset, we are more likely to engage in healthy behaviours such as regular exercise, a balanced diet, and adequate rest, all of which contribute to better physical health.

Additionally, a positive mindset opens us up to a world of possibilities. When we believe in ourselves and our abilities, we are more willing to take risks, explore new opportunities, and step outside our comfort zones. This mindset encourages us to embrace change, seize opportunities, and pursue our goals and dreams with enthusiasm and determination. By cultivating a positive mindset, we expand our horizons and create a fulfilling life aligned with our aspirations.

Understanding the power of a positive mindset requires acknowledging that it is not about denying or ignoring the challenges and hardships of life. Instead, it is about choosing to focus on the positive aspects, finding meaning in adversity, and responding to difficulties with resilience and optimism. A positive mindset empowers us to shape our reality and create a life that is filled with happiness, fulfillment, and a deep appreciation for the present moment.

The science behind conditioning the mind for positivity is rooted in the fields of neuroscience, psychology, and cognitive behavioural therapy. These disciplines provide valuable insights into how our thoughts, emotions, and behaviours are interconnected, offering a framework for understanding and harnessing the power of a positive mindset.

A positive mindset is an ever-present force, weaving its threads through the fabric of our existence. Having a positive mindset is not always easy; it requires us to let go of familiar patterns and step into the unknown. Yet, within this dance of transformation lies immense power and potential for personal growth.

Picture yourself standing on the precipice of change, looking into the vast horizon of possibilities. It may be a desire to break free from unhealthy habits, explore new passions, or embark on a journey of self-discovery. Whatever the catalyst, embracing change is about shifting our perspective and adopting a growth mindset.

A positive mindset is the belief that our abilities, intelligence, and talents can be developed through dedication, effort, and learning. It is a mindset that sees challenges as opportunities for growth, setbacks as stepping stones to success, and obstacles as invitations to push beyond our comfort zones. By embracing this mindset, we open ourselves up to the transformative power of change.

Change begins with self-reflection and a deep understanding of our desires and aspirations. Take a moment to listen to the whispers of your heart, to uncover the yearnings that have been tucked away amidst the demands of daily life. What dreams have you postponed? What passions have you neglected? Embrace change by acknowledging these desires and committing to pursue them with unwavering determination.

A positive mindset often challenges our sense of identity and disrupts the familiar patterns that have provided comfort and security. It's natural to feel a sense of unease or fear as you step outside your comfort zone. However, personal growth lies just beyond the boundaries of familiarity. Embrace change by acknowledging these fears but refusing to let them dictate your path. Channel your energy towards building resilience and cultivating the courage to move forward.

A positive mindset is not a linear process but rather a series of small steps and moments of transformation. Break down your goals into manageable tasks and celebrate each milestone along the way. Acknowledge that progress may be accompanied by setbacks and hurdles. Embrace change by viewing these challenges as opportunities for self-reflection, learning, and adaptation. Every stumble becomes an invaluable lesson that propels you further along your journey.

Seek out new experiences, broaden your horizons, and explore uncharted territories. Embrace change by embracing curiosity, open-mindedness, and a willingness to learn. Step outside your comfort zone, whether trying a new hobby, learning a new skill, or connecting with different cultures and perspectives. Embrace change by seeing every encounter as an opportunity for growth, expanding your understanding of the world and yourself.

Embrace a positive mindset with open arms, for it is through change that we evolve, learn, and become the best version of ourselves. Adopt a growth mindset, view challenges as stepping stones, and honour the call of your innermost desires. Embrace change, for within its embrace lies the transformative power that will shape your journey toward personal growth and fulfilment.

Reframing negative experiences involves finding empowering and constructive perspectives when faced with adversity or setbacks. It is about shifting our mindset and looking for alternative ways to interpret challenging situations. One approach is to look for lessons or opportunities for growth within the adversity. Consider what you can learn from the experience or how it can contribute to your personal development. By reframing setbacks as valuable learning experiences, you can extract wisdom and find motivation to keep moving forward.

We need to focus on the potential for positive outcomes or silver linings. We could ask ourselves, "What good can come out of this situation?" or "How can I turn this setback into an opportunity?" We can cultivate a more optimistic and resilient mindset by identifying and embracing the potential benefits.

We need to consider the bigger picture and how the negative experience fits into the context of our life's journey. Sometimes, setbacks can redirect us towards paths more aligned with our goals and aspirations. Reflect on whether the setback might guide you towards a different and potentially better path.

We need to challenge any self-limiting beliefs that arise from negative experiences. Instead of viewing setbacks as evidence of personal failure or inadequacy, recognize that they are a normal part of life and do not define your worth or abilities. Reframe the experience as an opportunity to challenge and overcome obstacles, reinforcing your resilience and inner strength.

A positive mindset involves finding empowering and constructive perspectives when faced with adversity or setbacks. It is about shifting our mindset and looking for alternative ways to interpret challenging situations. One approach is to look for lessons or opportunities for growth within the adversity. Consider what you can learn from the experience or how it can contribute to your personal development. By reframing setbacks as valuable learning experiences, you can extract wisdom and find motivation to keep moving forward.

We need to focus on the potential for positive outcomes or silver linings. We could ask ourselves, "What good can come out of this situation?" or "How can I turn this setback into an opportunity?" We can cultivate a more optimistic and resilient mindset by identifying and embracing the potential benefits.

We need to consider the bigger picture and how the negative experience fits into the context of our life's journey. Sometimes, setbacks can redirect us towards paths more aligned with our goals and aspirations. Reflect on whether the setback might guide you towards a different and potentially better path.

We need to challenge any self-limiting beliefs that arise from negative experiences. Instead of viewing setbacks as evidence of personal failure or inadequacy, recognize that they are a normal part of life and do not define your worth or abilities. Reframe the experience as an opportunity to challenge and overcome obstacles, reinforcing your resilience and inner strength.

We should explore cultivating gratitude, which involves fostering a mindset that focuses on the positive aspects of life and appreciating the things we often take for granted. By practicing gratitude, we can shift our perspective from lacking or negative to what we have and the positive experiences we encounter.

Incorporating a daily gratitude practice into our routine is important to change negative thought patterns and behaviours developing a positive mindset. Take a few moments each day to reflect on and write down things you are grateful for. It could be as simple as a beautiful sunset, a supportive friend, or a delicious meal. Cultivating gratitude requires conscious effort and regular practice.

Look for gratitude in small moments throughout the day. Notice the little things that bring you joy, such as a kind gesture from a stranger, the sound of birds chirping, or the warmth of a cup of tea. You can increase your overall sense of gratitude by actively paying attention to these moments.

Shift your focus from what's missing to what's present. Often, we tend to focus on what we lack or what went wrong. Instead, consciously redirect your attention to the abundance in your life. Acknowledge the positive experiences, relationships, and opportunities you have been blessed with.

When facing challenges or setbacks, try to find silver linings or lessons within them. Reflect on how difficult experiences have shaped you, taught you resilience, or provided new insights. Shifting your perspective to see the growth potential in adversity can foster a sense of gratitude for the lessons learned.

Express your gratitude to others. Take the time to let people know how much you appreciate them and their contributions to your life. It can be a heartfelt thank-you note, a kind word, or a simple act of kindness. Expressing gratitude benefits the receiver and deepens your sense of appreciation.

Practice a positive mindset. Recognize and appreciate your strengths, accomplishments, and efforts. Celebrate your progress and the steps you have taken toward personal growth. Treat yourself with kindness and acknowledge your value and worth.

Engage in acts of kindness and service. Giving back to others can cultivate a sense of gratitude and fulfilment. Volunteer your time, lend a helping hand, or engage in random acts of kindness. By extending kindness to others, you not only make a positive impact on their lives but also deepen your sense of gratitude.

Remember that a positive mindset is a practice that requires consistent effort and mindfulness. It may not always come naturally, especially during challenging times. Still, by intentionally cultivating gratitude, you can shift your focus toward the positive aspects of life, foster a sense of appreciation, and enhance your overall well-being.

Cultivating a positive mindset is essential as much as self-gratitude. Developing self-compassion is a process that involves cultivating kindness, understanding, and acceptance towards oneself. It requires recognizing our struggles, flaws, and imperfections and offering ourselves the same compassion and care we would extend to a dear friend or loved one. Here are some steps to help develop self-compassion:

We need to take the time to observe our thoughts, emotions, and reactions without judgment. Notice the times when we are being self-critical or harsh towards ourselves. This awareness is the first step towards practicing self-compassion.

A positive mindset challenge and reframe self-critical thoughts. When we notice self-critical thoughts arising, we must ask ourselves if we would say the same things to a friend in a similar situation. Often, the answer is no. Learn to treat yourself with the same kindness and understanding you would offer someone else. Reframe negative self-talk into more compassionate and supportive language.

Develop a self-compassion mantra or affirmation that resonates with you. This can be a simple phrase such as "I am deserving of love and kindness," or "I am enough as I am," or "I am in control," or "I am born to be a champion." Repeat this mantra to yourself during challenging moments or times of self-doubt, allowing it to anchor you in self-compassion and remind you of your inherent worth.

A positive mindset incorporates self-care regularly. Engage in activities that nurture your physical, emotional, spiritual and mental well-being. This can include exercise, healthy eating, getting enough rest, engaging in hobbies you enjoy, and seeking support from loved ones. Prioritize self-care as an essential part of your life.

Cultivate a non-judgmental attitude towards your mistakes and failures. Understand that making mistakes is a natural part of growth and learning. Treat yourself with understanding and kindness when things don't go as planned. Instead of dwelling on the past, focus on what you can learn from the experience and how to grow from it.

Practice self-compassion meditation. Set aside dedicated time for meditation focused on self-compassion. During this practice, direct loving-kindness and compassion towards yourself. Visualize yourself surrounded by love, warmth, and acceptance. Offer yourself kind and gentle words of support, acknowledging your struggles and affirming your worth.

Remember that developing self-compassion is a journey that takes time and practice. Be patient and gentle with yourself as you cultivate this new way of relating to yourself. Embrace imperfection and embrace self-compassion as an ongoing practice to bring healing, resilience, and a more profound sense of self-love into your life.

A positive mindset involves engaging in positive self-talk, which is also very important to consider in challenging negative thoughts which can lead to negative behaviours. It consists in harnessing the power of positive affirmations and consciously reframing our thoughts and beliefs. It is about intentionally cultivating a more optimistic and supportive inner dialogue.

We need to start by becoming aware of our inner critic. Notice the negative thoughts or self-limiting beliefs that arise in our minds. We must consider how these thoughts make us feel and impact our self-esteem and confidence.

Once we have identified negative self-talk patterns, challenge them with positive affirmations. Affirmations are positive statements that reflect the reality we want to create or the qualities we want to embody. We must repeat these affirmations to ourselves regularly, with conviction and belief. For example, if you struggle with self-doubt, you can affirm, "I am capable and deserving of success."

Reframe negative thoughts into more positive and constructive ones. Whenever a negative thought arises, we can consciously challenge it by asking ourselves if there's an alternative, more empowering perspective. For example, if you catch yourself thinking, "I always mess things up," reframe it as "I am learning and growing from every experience."

We need to practice self-compassion in our self-talk. Treat ourselves with kindness, understanding, and patience. Instead of berating ourselves for mistakes or perceived shortcomings, offer encouragement and support. We must remind ourselves that making mistakes is a natural part of learning and that we deserve love and compassion.

We need to be mindful of the language we use when talking to ourselves while maintaining a positive mindset. We should be choosing words that are uplifting, empowering, and supportive. We should avoid using negative or harsh language that reinforces self-doubt or self-criticism. Let's cultivate a positive and nurturing tone in our self-talk.

Visualization also can be a powerful tool to enhance positive self-talk. We can create mental images of ourselves succeeding, achieving our goals, and embodying the qualities we aspire to have. As we visualize, we can reinforce these images with positive affirmations. This practice helps us "Embrace Imperfections" and align our thoughts with a more positive self-perception.

We must surround ourselves with positive influences and seek individuals, books, or resources to inspire and uplift us. We must engage in conversations or activities that foster positivity and encourage self-belief. Surrounding ourselves with positive influences can support and reinforce our positive self-talk.

Consistency is critical when it comes to engaging in positive self-talk. Make it a habit to practice positive affirmations and reframe negative thoughts consistently. Over time, with this practice, we can "Embrace Imperfections" to naturally lean towards positive self-talk and foster a more optimistic and empowering mindset.

Remember that engaging in positive self-talk is a process that requires effort and mindfulness. It may take time to shift deeply ingrained patterns of negative self-talk, but with persistence and patience, you can cultivate a more positive and supportive inner dialogue. We can enhance our self-esteem, confidence, and overall well-being by harnessing the power of positive self-talk.

A positive mindset can be considered another outlet to challenge our negative thoughts and behaviours. It involves prioritizing activities that nurture our mental and emotional well-being, promoting a positive outlook and overall sense of balance in life. It is about intentionally setting aside time and energy to care for ourselves.

We need to recognize the importance of a positive mindset and the impact it has on our mental and psychological well-being. Understand that being positive is not selfish but necessary for overall health and happiness. Embrace the belief that you deserve to prioritize your needs and engage in activities that bring you joy and rejuvenation.

We need to identify activities that replenish and energize us. A positive mindset can take many forms, unique to each individual. It could be engaging in hobbies you love, spending time in nature, practicing mindfulness or meditation, reading a book, taking a relaxing bath, or simply enjoying quality time with loved ones. Discover what activities bring you a sense of peace, fulfilment, and relaxation.

We can create self-care as a means of a positive mindset routine. Set aside dedicated time each day or week for self-care activities. We must treat these moments as non-negotiable and prioritize them in our schedule. We should consider them as essential appointments with ourselves. This routine can help us establish a healthy balance and ensure that self-care becomes a consistent practice.

Nurturing our physical well-being through self-care is essential. We need to exercise regularly, prioritize healthy eating habits, get enough sleep, and listen to our body's needs. Taking care of our physical health contributes to our overall well-being and promotes a positive outlook.

We need to set boundaries and learn to say no. Prioritizing our own needs and learning to say no to commitments or requests that may overwhelm us or drain our energy. Creating healthy boundaries allows us to protect our time and energy, giving us more space for self-care activities.

We should practice self-compassion as part of our self-care routine and treat ourselves with kindness and understanding. We need to accept that we are not perfect and that it is okay to have limitations or make mistakes. We must embrace self-compassion in moments of difficulty or self-criticism, offering ourselves words of love and encouragement.

We should regularly reassess and adjust our self-care routine as needed. Our needs and circumstances may change over time, so it's essential to periodically evaluate our self-care practices and adapt accordingly. We need to listen to our intuition and be open to exploring new activities or approaches to self-care that resonate with us.

We must remember that a positive mindset is not a luxury but a necessity. By prioritizing positive mindset activities, we can invest in our mental and emotional well-being, promoting a positive outlook and a healthier relationship with ourselves and others. We should embrace a positive mindset as an ongoing practice supporting our overall happiness and fulfilment.

Let us embrace the idea that setbacks and obstacles are a natural part of growth. If we encounter challenges or temporarily veer off track, we can offer ourselves understanding and kindness. Use these moments as opportunities to learn, adjust, and recommit to our goals with renewed determination.

Our quest for self-mastery can continue as we engage in deep self-reflection. Through journaling and introspection, we can venture into the depths of our psyche, unravelling the underlying motivations behind our impulsive behaviour. This introspective journey serves as a compass, illuminating the path to lasting change.

With emotional regulation skills as our steadfast companions, we can equip ourselves with practical strategies to manage and regulate our emotions. These invaluable tools will allow us to navigate the stormy seas of life with grace and composure, reducing the likelihood of impulsive reactions that may hinder our progress.

Patience can become our ally as we embrace the art of delayed gratification. We can hone our ability to resist immediate temptations in favour of long-term benefits and personal growth. Through this practice, we can sow the seeds of discipline and fortitude, nurturing a resilient spirit that withstands the allure of impulsive choices.

We can harness the power of positive reinforcement to reinforce our commitment and dedication. By implementing techniques that reward and reinforce desired behaviours, we can lay a solid foundation for lasting change. We can discover the joy of celebrating small victories, cultivating a sense of accomplishment and motivation that propels us forward.

As we approach the culmination of our transformative journey, we craft a structured action plan—a roadmap that redirects our impulsive tendencies toward healthier alternatives. With a clear direction and unwavering resolve, we navigate the complexities of life, charting a course that aligns with our most authentic aspirations.

We can revel in the beauty of self-control, and as we celebrate those moments, no matter how small, we exercise restraint and demonstrate self-control. In these triumphs, we can find the fuel to propel us further along the path of self-discovery and growth, knowing that we possess the strength and resilience to conquer our impulsive impulses.

With each step we take each lesson we learn, we move closer to a life guided by intention and empowered choice. Let us embark on this journey together, embracing the transformation that awaits us as we learn to stop ourselves and step into a brighter future.

To gain control over a positive mindset, the first crucial step is to become keenly aware of the triggers that set off a chain reaction of impulsive or destructive behaviours within us. These triggers can take various forms, ranging from external circumstances to internal thoughts and emotions. By closely examining and identifying these triggers, we empower ourselves to intervene before they hijack our rationality and steer us off course.

A positive mindset is often tied to specific situations or environments that provoke impulsive reactions. For some, it might be the sight of a particular substance or object that triggers an irresistible craving. Others might find themselves vulnerable to impulsive behaviours when faced with social pressures or specific social settings. By paying attention to the external factors that consistently elicit impulsive responses, we can proactively devise strategies to navigate these triggers more effectively.

Equally significant are the internal triggers that reside within our thoughts and emotions. Negative self-talk, self-doubt, or feelings of inadequacy can be potent catalysts for impulsive actions. Similarly, intense emotions such as anger, sadness, or stress can overwhelm our rational thinking, leading us down a path of impulsive behaviour. By honing our self-awareness, we can detect the subtle cues that indicate the presence of these internal triggers, allowing us to intercept and disrupt their influence.

A positive mindset is essential to engage in a process of honest introspection and reflection. This may involve keeping a journal or diary to document instances when we find ourselves giving in to impulsivity. By reviewing these entries, patterns may emerge, providing valuable insights into the triggers that consistently precede impulsive behaviours. Additionally, seeking guidance from therapists, counsellors, or support groups can offer an outside perspective and help shed light on triggers that might be less apparent to us.

In this exploration, it is essential to approach the process without judgment or self-criticism. Recognizing triggers is not about placing blame or labelling ourselves negatively; instead, it is a compassionate and empowering act of self-discovery. By understanding the circumstances, thoughts, or emotions that ignite our impulsive tendencies, we gain the power to choose a different course of action.

A positive mindset is crucial to remain patient and persistent. Triggers may not always be immediately apparent; uncovering them may require time and reflection. It is a process of peeling back the layers of our experiences and emotions to reveal the root causes of our impulsive behaviours.

Ultimately, by recognizing a need for a positive mindset, we gain the ability to anticipate and intercept impulsive urges before they escalate. Armed with this knowledge, we can develop personalized strategies and coping mechanisms to navigate these triggers more effectively. By taking control of our responses and breaking the automatic cycle of impulsivity, we pave the way for healthier and more intentional choices, leading us towards a life of greater fulfilment and well-being.

A positive mindset profoundly impacts our thoughts, behaviours, and overall well-being. They possess the power to propel us toward impulsive actions or guide us toward thoughtful and deliberate choices. We need to develop our emotional intelligence as a critical skill to master.

At its core, emotional intelligence is the ability to recognize, understand, and manage our own emotions and the emotions of others. It encompasses a range of competencies, including self-awareness, self-regulation, empathy, and effective communication. By honing these skills, we equip ourselves with the tools to navigate the tumultuous terrain of intense emotions and prevent them from driving us toward impulsive actions.

The first step in harnessing emotional intelligence is cultivating self-awareness. It involves developing a deep understanding of our emotions, recognizing their triggers, and acknowledging how they influence our thoughts and behaviours. This heightened self-awareness allows us to catch ourselves in the grip of intense emotions before they propel us toward impulsive reactions.

It is the art of managing our intense emotions; we can respond thoughtfully and effectively rather than reacting impulsively. Self-regulation involves recognizing and acknowledging our emotions without being overwhelmed by them. We can learn to pause, take a step back, and consciously choose our responses, even in the face of intense emotional storms. This practice enables us to regain control over our actions and make decisions aligned with our long-term goals and values.

A positive mindset is a crucial element of emotional intelligence that supports our journey towards stopping impulsive behaviours. Empathy involves the ability to understand and share the feelings of others. By developing empathy, we cultivate a deeper understanding of the perspectives, needs, and emotions of those around us. This understanding helps us navigate interpersonal relationships with compassion and sensitivity, reducing the likelihood of impulsive reactions driven by misunderstandings or unchecked emotions.

Effective communication is an essential skill that complements a positive mindset. It involves expressing our emotions and needs in a clear and constructive manner while also being receptive to the feelings and needs of others. By honing our communication skills, we create an environment that encourages open dialogue, understanding, and collaborative problem-solving. This fosters healthier interactions and reduces the likelihood of impulsive outbursts or miscommunications that can lead to regrettable actions.

As we develop a positive mindset, it is essential to remember that it is a lifelong journey. It requires patience, practice, and a willingness to learn and grow continually. By investing time and effort into developing emotional intelligence, we lay the foundation for a more balanced and mindful approach to managing intense emotions. We gain the ability to recognize the warning signs of impulsivity and to choose responses that align with our values and long-term well-being.

Harnessing a positive mindset is a powerful tool to stop ourselves from succumbing to impulsive actions. By developing self-awareness, self-regulation, empathy, and effective communication, we gain the capacity to understand and manage intense emotions that can drive impulsive behaviours. With a positive mindset as our guide, we navigate the complex landscape of emotions with grace and intention, forging a path toward a more fulfilling and purposeful life.

In pursuing a positive mindset, positive reinforcement emerges as a powerful tool to reshape our behaviours and strengthen our resolve. By understanding the principles of positive reinforcement and implementing them in our lives, we can pave the way for lasting change and growth.

A positive mindset involves the deliberate use of rewards or incentives to encourage and reinforce desired behaviours. It operates on the premise that when a behaviour is followed by a positive consequence, such as a reward or recognition, the likelihood of that behaviour being repeated in the future increases. In essence, we train our minds to associate the desired behaviour with pleasurable outcomes, motivating us to continue making conscious choices.

One effective technique in utilizing a positive mindset is to identify and define specific behaviours that align with our goals and values. By clearly defining what constitutes a desired behaviour, we create a tangible target to aim for. This clarity enables us to recognize and appreciate our progress and make adjustments.

We must identify meaningful and personalized rewards that resonate with us to implement a positive mindset. These rewards can take various forms, such as treats or indulgences, quality time with loved ones, engaging in a favourite hobby, or even acknowledging our achievements through self-affirmation. The key is to select rewards that are personally meaningful and serve as incentives for us to stay on track.

Consistency is paramount when utilizing a positive mindset. By consistently and promptly providing rewards for desired behaviours, we reinforce the connection between our actions and the positive outcomes they bring. This consistency strengthens the neural pathways in our brains, making it easier for us to choose the desired behaviours over impulsive actions in the future.

In addition to immediate rewards, we can also implement delayed or cumulative reinforcement. Delayed reinforcement involves rewarding ourselves after successfully maintaining desired behaviours over a certain period. This approach helps us develop patience and the ability to delay gratification, which is essential for long-term personal growth.

A positive mindset involves tracking and celebrating our progress over time and accumulating rewards for consistent effort and improvement. This technique allows us to acknowledge and appreciate the incremental steps we take on our journey, reinforcing our commitment to change.

It is important to note that a positive mindset should not be seen as a means of punishment or judgment for our past impulsive actions. Instead, it is a compassionate and empowering approach that focuses on acknowledging and nurturing the positive changes we make in the present. By shifting our focus to the desired behaviours we want to reinforce, we create a supportive and growth-oriented environment within ourselves.

As we implement a positive mindset, we gradually "Embrace Imperfections" and cultivate a mindset that embraces conscious choices and self-control. We learn to associate the rewards and positive outcomes with the behaviours that serve our higher goals and aspirations. Over time, these reinforced behaviours can become ingrained in our daily lives, replacing impulsive actions with intentional, mindful decision-making.

In pursuing a positive mindset, by rewiring the brain, creating an action plan becomes an indispensable tool on our transformative journey. An action plan serves as a roadmap, guiding us towards healthier alternatives and redirecting our impulsive tendencies onto a path of growth and self-improvement.

We lay the groundwork for a focused and effective action plan by clearly identifying the impulsive tendencies that hinder our progress. This clarity allows us to target our efforts and channel our energy toward the areas that require our attention the most. We need first to define our goals and aspirations. We may want to ask ourselves, "What are the specific behaviours we seek to change?"

Once we have identified our goals, it is essential to break them down into smaller, manageable steps. This step-by-step approach enables us to progress incrementally, providing a sense of accomplishment and motivation. By setting realistic and achievable milestones, we cultivate a sense of empowerment and build momentum towards lasting change.

In developing a positive mindset, it is vital to explore and research alternative behaviours that align with our desired outcomes. What healthier choices can we make when faced with impulsive urges? Are there specific strategies or coping mechanisms that resonate with our values and strengths? When we explore these possibilities, we expand our repertoire of options and arm ourselves with the tools needed to navigate challenging moments.

Accountability plays a crucial role in the effectiveness of a positive mindset. We may seek support from trusted friends, family members, or professionals who can provide guidance and hold us accountable for our commitments. Sharing our intentions and progress with others creates a network of support and encouragement, bolstering our motivation and providing valuable feedback.

As we implement a positive mindset, it is essential to remain flexible and adaptable. We may encounter setbacks or obstacles that test our resolve. In these moments, we must be willing to reassess our strategies, make necessary adjustments, and learn from our experiences. Embracing a positive mindset allows us to view setbacks as opportunities for growth and development, reinforcing our determination to succeed.

Regular evaluation and reflection are integral components of a positive mindset. By periodically assessing our progress, we can celebrate the milestones achieved, acknowledge areas for improvement, and refine our approach as needed. Self-reflection provides insights into our patterns and triggers, allowing us to make informed choices and further refine our action plans.

Throughout this process, it is crucial to cultivate self-compassion and kindness towards ourselves. A positive mindset is a journey that requires patience and understanding. It is natural to encounter moments of difficulty or relapse. By treating ourselves with compassion and refraining from self-judgment, we create a nurturing environment for growth and increase our resilience in the face of challenges while developing a positive mindset.

Celebrating the achievements and moments of a positive mindset becomes an essential part of our action plan. Every small victory, no matter how seemingly insignificant, deserves recognition. By acknowledging and celebrating our progress, we reinforce positive behaviours and boost our confidence, fuelling our motivation to continue on the path of self-improvement.

In creating a positive mindset to redirect impulsive tendencies towards healthier alternatives, we lay the foundation for transformative change. By deliberately cultivating new habits and choices, we reclaim our power and forge a path toward a more balanced and fulfilling life. We need to be determined resilient, and carry an unwavering commitment to a positive mindset

Sustaining positive change begins with a deep-rooted commitment to yourself. Recognize the significance of your progress and reaffirm your dedication to a healthier and more fulfilling life.

Embrace the belief that you can maintain this positive trajectory and deserve the happiness and well-being that come with it.

We must develop strategies to support our long-term success with a positive mindset. We must reflect on the practices and routines that have helped us share our self-destructive habits thus far. Identify the triggers and temptations that can pull us back into old patterns and devise strategies to mitigate their influence. This could involve creating a supportive environment, surrounding ourselves with positive influences, and establishing boundaries to protect our progress.

We should establish healthy habits as a solid framework to sustain a positive mindset. Consistency is vital, as it solidifies new behaviours and minimizes the likelihood of slipping back into old patterns. We should integrate these habits into our daily routine, making them a non-negotiable part of our lives. Whether it's dedicating time to exercise, preparing nutritious meals, practicing mindfulness, or seeking moments of self-care, commit to these habits wholeheartedly.

Find joy in the journey. Sustaining a positive mindset is not just about maintaining discipline; it's about embracing the beauty of the process itself. Celebrate the small victories, relish in the progress you continue to make, and savour the moments of growth and self-discovery along the way. Cultivate gratitude for the opportunity to transform your life and let it fuel your determination to stay the course.

As discussed earlier, we must embrace a growth mindset that views challenges as opportunities for learning and growth. Recognize that setbacks are a natural part of any journey and see them as stepping stones rather than roadblocks. When faced with obstacles, assess them objectively, extract the lessons they hold, and use them to further refine your strategies for sustaining positive change.

Above all, be kind and patient with yourself. Recognize that maintaining a positive mindset is a lifelong commitment, and there may be times when you stumble or falter. Embrace these moments as opportunities for growth and self-compassion. Learn to forgive yourself, recalibrate, and recommit to your journey. Remember that every day is a fresh start—a chance to reaffirm your dedication and continue the legacy of positive change you have begun.

A positive mindset is an ever-present force, weaving its threads through the fabric of our existence. Embracing a positive mindset is not always easy; it requires letting go of familiar patterns and stepping into the unknown. Yet, within this dance of transformation lies immense power and potential for personal growth.

Picture yourself standing on the precipice of change, looking into the vast horizon of possibilities. It may be a desire to break free from unhealthy habits, explore new passions, or embark on a journey of self-discovery. Whatever the catalyst, embracing change is about shifting our perspective and adopting a growth mindset.

A positive mindset is the belief that our abilities, intelligence, and talents can be developed through dedication, effort, and learning. It is a mindset that sees challenges as opportunities for growth, setbacks as stepping stones to success, and obstacles as invitations to push beyond our comfort zones. By embracing this mindset, we open ourselves up to the transformative power of change.

A positive mindset begins with self-reflection and a deep understanding of our desires and aspirations. Take a moment to listen to the whispers of your heart, to uncover the yearnings that have been tucked away amidst the demands of daily life. What dreams have you postponed? What passions have you neglected? Embrace change by acknowledging these desires and committing to pursue them with unwavering determination.

As you embark on this journey, be prepared to encounter resistance. A positive mindset often challenges our sense of identity and disrupts the familiar patterns that have provided comfort and security. It's natural to feel a sense of unease or fear as you step outside your comfort zone. However, personal growth lies just beyond the boundaries of familiarity. Embrace a positive mindset by acknowledging these fears but refusing to let them dictate your path. Channel your energy towards building resilience and cultivating the courage to move forward.

A positive mindset is not a linear process but rather a series of small steps and moments of transformation. Break down your goals into manageable tasks and celebrate each milestone along the way. Acknowledge that progress may be accompanied by setbacks and hurdles. Embrace a positive mindset by viewing these challenges as opportunities for self-reflection, learning, and adaptation. Every stumble becomes an invaluable lesson that propels you further along your journey.

Seek out new experiences, broaden your horizons, and explore uncharted territories. Embrace a positive mindset by embracing curiosity, open-mindedness, and a willingness to learn. Step outside your comfort zone, whether trying a new hobby, learning a new skill, or connecting with different cultures and perspectives. Embrace a positive mindset by seeing every encounter as an opportunity for growth, expanding your understanding of the world and yourself.

Embrace a positive mindset with open arms, for it is through change that we evolve, learn, and become the best version of ourselves. Adopt a growth mindset, view challenges as stepping stones, and honour the call of your innermost desires. Embrace a positive mindset, for within its embrace lies the transformative power that will shape your journey toward personal growth and fulfilment.

SELF-DESTRUCTIVE
BEHAVIOURS

Self-destructive behaviours can develop from bad habits, abuse, traumas, addictions, toxic relationships and a negative past, which can often lead us to grapple with self-destructive behaviours that hinder our progress. These habits, ingrained over time, keep us from reaching our full potential and experiencing the fulfilling life we desire. It's time to break free from the shackles of these destructive patterns and embark on a transformative path of shedding bad habits.

Letting go of self-destructive behaviours means digging deep into the intricacies of identifying and overcoming the habits that impede our growth. We must explore the underlying causes behind these behaviours and equip ourselves with practical strategies to break free from their hold.

Recognizing that change from self-destructive behaviours can be challenging, we need to embark on this journey with compassion and embrace our imperfections, acknowledging that personal growth is a continuous process. By shedding these self-destructive habits, we pave the way for positive transformations that align with our true potential.

We can learn how to cultivate self-awareness, create healthier habits, seek support from others who understand our struggles and embrace change as a catalyst for personal growth. Each step brings us closer to a happier and more fulfilling future, where we can thrive without the burdens of self-destructive behaviours.

We must cast aside the chains of our old habits and embrace a life that aligns with our deepest aspirations. By shedding these bad habits, we empower ourselves to live authentically and create a future filled with joy, purpose, and limitless possibilities.

We may have always dreamed of living a fulfilling and joyful life. However, there may be things holding us back—self-destructive behaviours that seem to lurk in the shadows. We may be unaware of the impact these habits are having on our personal growth and happiness.

If we take some time to reflect, we may notice patterns of behaviour that have led to adverse outcomes. Self-realization should be a turning point where we can decide that it is time to confront these self-destructive behaviours and reclaim control over personal well-being.

Identifying harmful habits may take a period of self-reflection and soul-searching, where we can explore the actions and choices that hindered progress and personal growth. It may require much courage and honesty to confront the truth. We need to be determined to break free from the chains of self-destruction.

Through this process, we may discover various self-destructive behaviours, including procrastination, excessive consumption of unhealthy substances, negative self-talk, and a tendency to sabotage relationships. Each revelation we bring may have a mix of emotions—regret, frustration, and a desire for change.

With newfound awareness, we can start observing the consequences of these behaviours. Relationships suffer, goals are left unfulfilled, and personal happiness seems elusive. The detrimental impact can become more precise, motivating us to take the necessary steps toward shedding these destructive habits.

Acknowledging the harmful habits is just the beginning. We need to understand that change requires dedication and effort. It meant stepping out of the comfort zone, challenging long-standing patterns, and embracing discomfort. However, the vision of a better, more fulfilling life serves as a beacon of hope and motivation.

We may seek guidance from mentors and friends who have overcome similar challenges, learning from our experiences and insights. We can share stories of resilience, inner strength, and the transformative power of shedding self-destructive behaviours. This support system can become an invaluable source of encouragement and accountability throughout our journey.

As we dig deeper into self-discovery, it will become evident that these self-destructive behaviours were rooted in deeper emotional wounds, fears, and insecurities. Recognizing this connection opens the door to a more compassionate understanding of oneself.

With every step taken on this transformative path, we can feel a sense of liberation and empowerment. Each small victory, like resisting the urge to engage in self-destructive behaviours or replacing them with healthier alternatives, brought a renewed sense of self-worth and strength.

The process of identifying self-destructive behaviours is not without its challenges. There will be moments of self-doubt and occasional setbacks along the way. However, through perseverance and a deep commitment to personal growth, Alex learned that every stumble was an opportunity for learning and growth.

When we continue to remove destructive habits, a newfound

sense of freedom and self-mastery emerges. Personal growth flourishes, and the journey becomes less about letting go of negative behaviours and more about embracing a positive and fulfilling life.

Through self-reflection, courage, and a commitment to personal growth, we can pave the way for a brighter future, freeing us from the shackles of self-destruction.

In shedding bad habits and embracing personal growth, it is crucial to understand the depths of our behaviours and their root causes. It is in this exploration that we gain profound insights into why we engage in self-destructive habits and what triggers them.

This introspective journey can lead us to a myriad of emotions and experiences that have shaped our behaviours over time. Each individual carries a unique set of circumstances, past traumas, beliefs, and influences that contribute to the formation of these habits.

Exploring the root causes requires digging deep into our past and present, examining the intricate web of factors influencing our choices. It may involve reflecting on our upbringing, relationships, societal pressures, and even our internal struggles. By doing so, we can unravel the complex tapestry of our lives and better understand why we engage in self-destructive behaviours.

During this process, we may uncover patterns and triggers that contribute to the repetition of these habits. It could be the result of unresolved emotional pain, a desire for control, a means of coping with stress, or a way to seek temporary relief. Whatever the underlying reasons may be, understanding them provides us with a roadmap to navigate the path toward positive change.

Through self-reflection, therapy, or seeking guidance from mentors, we can gradually unravel the layers that obscure the root causes of our self-destructive behaviours. We can learn to confront our fears, acknowledge our vulnerabilities, and gain clarity on the deeper needs that drive our actions. This newfound awareness empowers us to break free from the shackles of our past and embark on a journey of transformation.

Understanding the root causes is not an easy task. It requires courage, vulnerability, and a willingness to face uncomfortable truths. It may be accompanied by moments of pain as we confront wounds that have long been buried within us. Yet, in these moments of discomfort lies the opportunity for profound growth and healing.

We must approach understanding the root causes with compassion and patience. It is not about placing blame or dwelling on past mistakes but instead seeking wisdom and insight to forge a brighter future.

By unravelling the tangled threads of our behaviours and gaining a deeper understanding of the root causes, we equip ourselves with the tools necessary for lasting change. Armed with this knowledge, we can navigate the journey of shedding bad habits with greater clarity, purpose, and resilience.

One crucial step is to break free from the repetitive patterns and cycles that keep us trapped in self-destructive behaviours. Breaking the cycle requires determination, resilience, and a commitment to personal growth. We must explore effective strategies to interrupt these harmful patterns and pave the way for positive change.

Understanding the triggers that lead to self-destructive behaviours is the first step in breaking the cycle. We can learn to identify the situations, emotions, or thoughts that often precede these behaviours, enabling us to intervene before falling into old patterns.

Surrounding ourselves with a supportive environment is essential for breaking the cycle. We can explore ways to foster a positive and encouraging atmosphere reinforcing our commitment to change. This may involve seeking the support of loved ones, joining support groups, or seeking guidance from mentors or professionals.

Self-destructive behaviours often serve as coping mechanisms for underlying issues. We can discover healthier alternatives to cope with stress, anxiety, or emotional pain, such as engaging in physical exercise, practicing relaxation techniques, or pursuing creative outlets.

Life can be a rollercoaster of emotions, filled with moments of joy, excitement, and fulfilment. However, there are also times when we face stress, vulnerability, and uncertainty. During these challenging moments, it is crucial to develop healthy coping mechanisms to navigate the stormy seas of our emotions and replace self-destructive behaviours with actions that promote well-being and resilience.

Imagine yourself in a moment of vulnerability, where the weight of the world feels heavy upon your shoulders. It could be a demanding work situation, a personal loss, or simply the overwhelming pressure of daily life. In times like these, it's easy to resort to self-destructive behaviours as a means of temporary relief or escape. However, developing healthy coping mechanisms offers a more sustainable path towards emotional balance and inner strength.

To embark on this transformative journey to *"Embrace Imperfections,"* begin by cultivating self-awareness. Take a gentle pause and tune in to your emotions, thoughts, and triggers. What are the patterns that emerge when stress or vulnerability arises? Are there self-destructive behaviours, such as excessive eating, substance abuse, or isolation, that you tend to gravitate towards? Acknowledging these patterns is the first step towards breaking free from their grip.

Once aware, actively seek healthy coping mechanisms that resonate with your values and support your well-being. It may be engaging in physical activities like yoga, running, or dancing, which release pent-up energy and boosts endorphins. Perhaps mindfulness and meditation can provide solace and help you find peace amidst the chaos. Alternatively, expressing yourself through creative outlets like painting, writing, or playing an instrument may serve as a cathartic release. Explore different options and find what resonates with you on a deep level.

Building healthy coping mechanisms is not an overnight process; it requires dedication and practice. Embrace each new technique with patience and an open mind. Start small and gradually incorporate these practices into your daily routine. When stress or vulnerability strikes, intentionally choose your healthy coping mechanism over self-destructive behaviours. Over time, these choices become ingrained habits that support your emotional well-being.

It's important to remember that developing healthy coping mechanisms doesn't mean avoiding or suppressing negative emotions. Instead, it's about acknowledging and accepting them as a natural part of the human experience. Allow yourself to sit with discomfort, and then consciously choose a healthy coping mechanism to constructively process and navigate those emotions. By doing so, you cultivate emotional resilience and equip yourself with tools to face life's challenges head-on.

Developing healthy coping mechanisms can become a turning point—an opportunity to embrace resilience, growth, and self-compassion. Replace self-destructive behaviours with activities that nurture your well-being. As you navigate the ebb and flow of stress and vulnerability, remember that you have the power to choose healthy responses to rewrite the narrative of how you cope with challenges. Each positive choice reinforces your inner strength and creates a healthier, more fulfilling path forward.

Cultivating mindfulness and self-awareness plays a pivotal role in breaking the cycle. By becoming more present in the moment, we can observe our thoughts, emotions, and behaviours without judgment. This awareness can empower us to make conscious choices and interrupt the automatic response of engaging in self-destructive behaviours.

Developing a resilience toolkit equips us with strategies to overcome challenges and temptations. We can explore techniques including positive self-talk, visualization, affirmations, and seeking inspiration from personal role models.

Breaking the cycle requires embracing change as an opportunity for growth. We can learn to shift our mindset from resistance to embracing the transformative power of change, recognizing that each step forward brings us closer to a healthier and more fulfilling life.

Establishing clear boundaries is crucial in breaking the cycle of self-destructive behaviours. We can explore how to set boundaries with ourselves and others, prioritizing our well-being and avoiding situations that may trigger our old patterns.

In some cases, breaking the cycle may require professional assistance. We can discuss the benefits of seeking therapy, counselling, or coaching to receive guidance, support, and specialized techniques tailored to our specific needs.

Relapses are a natural part of shedding bad habits. We can explore how to approach relapses with compassion and use them as opportunities for learning and growth rather than as reasons to give up.

Throughout the process of breaking the cycle, it's essential to acknowledge and celebrate our progress, no matter how small. We can learn the significance of celebrating milestones, as they reinforce our commitment and motivation to continue toward positive change. By implementing these strategies and adopting a resilient mindset, we can interrupt the patterns and cycles of self-destructive behaviours, paving the way for a healthier, more fulfilling life. Let's embark on this transformative journey of shedding bad habits and embracing personal growth together.

One crucial step that paves the way for lasting change is cultivating self-awareness. It is an empowering process of introspection and self-reflection that allows us to delve deep within ourselves and gain a profound understanding of our behaviours and tendencies.

In pursuing personal growth, developing self-awareness can become an essential compass that guides us toward shedding self-destructive habits. It requires us to peel back the layers and examine our thoughts, emotions, and actions with a keen and unbiased eye.

To cultivate self-awareness, we must create moments of quiet introspection, away from the noise and distractions of everyday life. In these moments of solitude, we can listen to the whispers of our inner voice, exploring the intricacies of our thoughts and emotions without judgment.

Through self-awareness, we can gain insight into the root causes of our self-destructive behaviours. We can uncover the triggers, patterns, and underlying reasons that have led us astray. We can unravel the layers of conditioning, fears, and insecurities contributing to our harmful habits with compassionate self-reflection.

As we deepen our self-awareness, we can develop the ability to recognize destructive tendencies as they arise. We can become attuned to the warning signs, the subtle cues that precede our self-sabotaging actions. This heightens our awareness that empowers us to pause, take a breath, and choose a different path.

Cultivating self-awareness is a gradual and ongoing process. It requires patience, curiosity, and a willingness to confront uncomfortable truths about ourselves. It is not about self-condemnation but rather about fostering self-compassion and a genuine desire for personal growth.

As we navigate the terrain of self-awareness, we may discover aspects of ourselves that we had long overlooked or dismissed. We may uncover hidden strengths, passions, and values that can serve as beacons of light on our path to transformation.

Through self-awareness, we can begin to reclaim ourselves, realizing that we have the power to rewrite our narrative and choose a different course. We can recognize that shedding bad habits is not a single act but a continuous process of self-discovery and growth.

Creating healthy habits is a transformative process of self-discovery and intentional choices that leads to a better and more vibrant life. It begins with a deep desire for change, a commitment to nurturing your body, soul (mind, will and emotions), and spirit.

It is essential to set clear and achievable goals. Take a moment to reflect on what areas of your life you wish to improve. Is it your physical fitness, nutrition, sleep routine, or stress management? Identify specific objectives that resonate with your aspirations, such as exercising three times a week or eating a balanced diet rich in fruits and vegetables. Clear goals serve as guideposts along your path, providing direction and motivation.

With goals in mind, it's time to design a plan of action. Break down your objectives into smaller, manageable steps. Perhaps you can start by scheduling regular workout sessions in your calendar or creating a meal plan for the week. Remember, Rome wasn't built in a day, and neither are healthy habits. Taking small, consistent actions can build momentum and pave the way for lasting change.

Now comes the challenging part: cultivating discipline and consistency. Habits are formed through repetition and practice. Commit to your plan and hold yourself accountable. It may require adjusting your schedule, making sacrifices, or overcoming moments of temptation. But remember, each choice you make aligns with your vision of a healthier life.

It is essential to embrace self-care. Nurturing your body, mind, and spirit is crucial for overall well-being. Prioritize quality sleep, carve out time for relaxation, engage in activities that bring you joy, and practice mindfulness. Remember that self-care is not selfish but an investment in vitality and happiness.

Acknowledge and appreciate the positive changes you've made. Treat yourself to rewards that align with your healthy lifestyle, such as a relaxing massage, a new workout outfit, or a day spent in nature. These small celebrations serve as reminders of your dedication and fuel your motivation to keep going.

Creating healthy habits is an ongoing dance between self-discovery, discipline, and self-care. Embrace the journey, and be patient with yourself. Know that each day presents an opportunity to make choices that support your well-being. Step by step, you'll build a foundation of healthy habits that will empower you to live a vibrant and fulfilling life.

In the pursuit of creating healthy habits, seeking support can be a transformative and empowering step. While personal motivation and determination are essential, having a solid support system can provide the guidance, encouragement, and accountability needed to navigate the challenges of shedding bad habits and embracing new, positive ones.

Imagine yourself standing at the crossroads, eager to embark on a journey towards a healthier and more fulfilling life. The path ahead may seem daunting, as old habits can be deeply ingrained and difficult to break. That's when the power of seeking support comes into play.

One way to seek support is by finding mentors or coaches who specialize in the areas you wish to improve. These knowledgeable individuals had walked the path before you, faced similar challenges, and acquired valuable insights. They can offer guidance tailored to your unique circumstances, helping you set realistic goals, develop effective strategies, and stay on track. A mentor or coach can provide a fresh perspective, encouraging you when self-doubt arises and celebrating your achievements as you progress towards your goals.

Support groups are a valuable resource, as they unite individuals with a shared desire for personal growth and well-being. Whether it's a fitness group, a nutrition club, or a mindfulness community, joining these supportive circles can create a sense of camaraderie and understanding. You can openly share your struggles and triumphs within these groups, knowing you're surrounded by individuals who genuinely empathize with your journey. Through shared experiences, you can gain inspiration, gather tips, and build meaningful connections that can last a lifetime.

The digital age has opened up a world of online support communities. Forums, social media groups, and wellness apps provide platforms to connect with like-minded individuals, regardless of geographic boundaries. These virtual spaces offer a wealth of resources, from educational content to daily challenges and discussions. Engaging in online communities can offer a sense of belonging and empower you with knowledge and inspiration from people on a similar path.

Seeking support is not a sign of weakness but rather a testament to your commitment to growth and improvement. It takes courage to reach out and ask for help. Remember, we are social beings, and human connection is vital for our well-being. By surrounding yourself with positive influences, you create an environment that nurtures your goals and reinforces your determination.

In your quest for healthier habits, embrace the power of seeking support. Find mentors or coaches who can guide you, connect with support groups that share your aspirations, and engage in online communities to expand your network. Together, they can provide the encouragement, guidance, and accountability you need to navigate the twists and turns of this transformative journey. With their help, you'll find strength in moments of doubt, celebrate milestones, and ultimately, emerge as a better and healthier version of yourself.

Personal growth and transforming yourself from negative experiences and self-destructive behaviours create the ability to take every step forward as a milestone worth celebrating. The journey of shedding bad habits is no exception. It is a transformative path that requires resilience, determination, and a willingness to embrace change. Along this winding road, it's essential to recognize and celebrate every ounce of progress, no matter how small it may seem.

Picture yourself on this journey, navigating the twists and turns of self-improvement. As you strive to shed old habits, there will be moments of triumph and moments of struggle. It's easy to get caught up in the overwhelming nature of the ultimate goal, losing sight of the significance of each small step forward. But remember, progress is not always measured by giant leaps but by the accumulation of consistent efforts.

Celebrate the moments when you resist the pull of old habits, those instances when you consciously choose a healthier path. It could be the first time you resist the temptation to reach for that sugary snack or the day you complete a workout, even when your motivation is waning. These seemingly insignificant moments are stepping stones towards lasting change and deserve recognition.

Take a pause and reflect on how far you've come. Look back at the person you were when you first embarked on this journey and compare it to who you are now. Celebrate the growth, the resilience, and the determination that have carried you to this point. Acknowledge the inner strength you've cultivated and the positive choices you've made along the way. Celebrate the person you are becoming.

It's also important to find joy in the small victories. Break down your ultimate goal into smaller milestones achievable in the shorter term. When you reach these milestones, no matter how modest they may be, take a moment to revel in your accomplishment. Treat yourself to something special—a small indulgence, a moment of relaxation, or a joyful activity that brings you happiness. These celebrations serve as reminders of your progress and fuel your motivation to keep going.

Remember that setbacks are a natural part of any journey. When you encounter obstacles or slip back into old habits, be compassionate with yourself. Instead of dwelling on perceived failures, focus on the lessons learned and the resilience gained from those experiences. Embrace setbacks as opportunities for growth and celebrate the resilience it takes to get back on track.

Share your milestones with those who support and uplift you. Let your loved ones in on your achievements, whether big or small. Their encouragement and celebration amplify your joy and validate the significance of your progress. Find solace in the community, whether it's a close friend, a support group, or an online community. Connect with others who understand your challenges and can offer support and cheer you on during each milestone.

In this journey towards shedding bad habits and regaining the strength from self-destructive behaviours, celebrating milestones becomes a crucial chapter—an ode to the progress made and a testament to your commitment to personal growth. Recognize the significance of each small step forward, rejoice in the moments of triumph, and cultivate a mindset of positivity and self-appreciation. With each milestone celebrated, you strengthen your resolve and reinforce the belief that you are capable of creating lasting change.

As the winds of change carry you forward on your journey of shedding self-destructive behaviours, there comes a crucial point where sustaining positive change becomes the focus. It is at this juncture that you lay the foundation for long-term success, establishing strategies and practices that will safeguard the progress you have made and propel you toward a brighter, healthier future.

Imagine yourself at this pivotal moment, standing on the precipice of a transformed life. The habits you once clung to, which held you back, have gradually given way to healthier choices and new behaviour patterns. But how do you ensure this newfound progress endures, becoming an intrinsic part of your identity rather than a fleeting change?

Sustaining positive change begins with a deep-rooted commitment to yourself. Recognize the significance of your progress and reaffirm your dedication to a healthier and more fulfilling life. Embrace the belief that you can maintain this positive trajectory and deserve the happiness and well-being that come with it.

We need to develop strategies that will support our long-term success. We must reflect on the practices and routines that have helped us share our self-destructive habits thus far. Identify the triggers and temptations that can pull us back into old patterns and devise strategies to mitigate their influence. This could involve creating a supportive environment, surrounding ourselves with positive influences, and establishing boundaries to protect our progress.

We should establish healthy habits as a solid framework for sustained positive change. Consistency is vital, as it solidifies new behaviours and minimizes the likelihood of slipping back into old patterns. We should integrate these habits into our daily routine, making them a non-negotiable part of our lives. Whether it's dedicating time to exercise, preparing nutritious meals, practicing mindfulness, or seeking moments of self-care, commit to these habits wholeheartedly.

Find joy in the journey. Sustaining positive change is not just about maintaining discipline; it's about embracing the beauty of the process itself. Celebrate the small victories, relish in the progress you continue to make, and savour the moments of growth and self-discovery along the way. Cultivate gratitude for the opportunity to transform your life and let it fuel your determination to stay the course.

As discussed earlier, we need to embrace a growth mindset that views challenges as opportunities for learning and growth. Recognize that setbacks are a natural part of any journey and see them as stepping stones rather than roadblocks. When faced with obstacles, assess them objectively, extract the lessons they hold, and use them to further refine your strategies for sustaining positive change.

Above all, be kind and patient with yourself. Recognize that sustaining positive change is a lifelong commitment, and there may be times when you stumble or falter. Embrace these moments as opportunities for growth and self-compassion. Learn to forgive yourself, recalibrate, and recommit to your journey. Remember that every day is a fresh start—a chance to reaffirm your dedication and continue the legacy of positive change you have begun.

Change is an ever-present force, weaving its threads through the fabric of our existence. Embracing change is not always easy; it requires us to let go of familiar patterns and step into the unknown. Yet, within this dance of transformation lies immense power and potential for personal growth.

Picture yourself standing on the precipice of change, looking into the vast horizon of possibilities. It may be a desire to break free from unhealthy habits, explore new passions, or embark on a journey of self-discovery. Whatever the catalyst, embracing change is about shifting our perspective and adopting a growth mindset.

To avoid self-destructive behaviours, we must believe that our abilities, intelligence, and talents can be developed through dedication, effort, and learning. It is a mindset that sees challenges as opportunities for growth, setbacks as stepping stones to success, and obstacles as invitations to push beyond our comfort zones. By embracing this mindset, we open ourselves up to the transformative power of change.

Change begins with self-reflection and a deep understanding of our desires and aspirations. Take a moment to listen to the whispers of your heart, to uncover the yearnings that have been tucked away amidst the demands of daily life. What dreams have you postponed? What passions have you neglected? Embrace change by acknowledging these desires and committing to pursue them with unwavering determination.

As you embark on this journey, be prepared to encounter resistance. Change often challenges our sense of identity and disrupts the familiar patterns that have provided comfort and security. It's natural to feel a sense of unease or fear as you step outside your comfort zone. However, personal growth lies just beyond the boundaries of familiarity. Embrace change by acknowledging these fears but refusing to let them dictate your path. Channel your energy towards building resilience and cultivating the courage to move forward.

Change is not a linear process but rather a series of small steps and moments of transformation. Break down your goals into manageable tasks and celebrate each milestone along the way. Acknowledge that progress may be accompanied by setbacks and hurdles. Embrace change by viewing these challenges as opportunities for self-reflection, learning, and adaptation. Every stumble becomes an invaluable lesson that propels you further along your journey.

Seek out new experiences, broaden your horizons, and explore uncharted territories. Embrace change by embracing curiosity, open-mindedness, and a willingness to learn. Step outside your comfort zone, whether trying a new hobby, learning a new skill, or connecting with different cultures and perspectives. Embrace change by seeing every encounter as an opportunity for growth, expanding your understanding of the world and yourself.

Embrace change with open arms, for it is through change that we evolve, learn, and become the best version of ourselves. Adopt a growth mindset, view challenges as stepping stones, and honour the call of your innermost desires. Embrace change, for within its embrace lies the transformative power that will shape your journey toward personal growth and fulfilment.

As we conclude this chapter on letting go of self-destructive behaviours, we do so with a deep sense of empowerment and hope. Throughout this transformative journey, we have taken courageous steps to identify and acknowledge the harmful habits hindering our personal growth. We have gained a profound understanding of the root causes and triggers behind these behaviours, allowing us to address them at their core.

Breaking the cycle of self-destructive behaviours has been a decisive step on our path to positive change. We have implemented strategies to interrupt the patterns and cycles that trap us in harmful patterns. We have paved the way for a brighter, more fulfilling future through perseverance and determination.

Cultivating self-awareness has played a pivotal role in our journey. We have developed a heightened self-awareness, enabling us to recognize and address our destructive tendencies. By understanding our triggers and vulnerabilities, we have gained the power to make conscious choices that support our well-being.

Creating healthy habits has been instrumental in our transformation. We have replaced negative behaviours with positive, life-enhancing habits that nurture our physical, emotional, and mental well-being. These new habits have become pillars of support, guiding us towards a more balanced and fulfilling life.

Seeking support has been crucial in our journey of letting go of self-destructive behaviours. We have reached out to mentors, coaches, or support groups that provide guidance, understanding, and accountability. Their presence has been instrumental in navigating the challenges and staying committed to our journey of positive change.

Embracing change has been a transformative process. We have opened ourselves to the power of transformation, adopting a growth mindset that encourages personal growth and evolution. With each step forward, we have embraced the limitless possibilities that lie ahead, knowing that change is an inherent part of our journey.

Discovering healthy coping mechanisms has been a vital aspect of our progress. We have found healthy ways to navigate times of stress or vulnerability, replacing self-destructive behaviours with strategies that promote well-being and resilience. By developing effective coping mechanisms, we have equipped ourselves with the tools to overcome challenges and maintain our positive trajectory.

Let us celebrate the milestones we have achieved along the way. No matter how small, each step forward is a testament to our strength and commitment to personal growth. By acknowledging and celebrating our progress, we reinforce our belief in our ability to sustain positive change.

Moving forward, we are committed to sustaining the positive change we have achieved. We understand the importance of establishing strategies and practices that will support us in the long run. With unwavering determination and a renewed sense of purpose, we embrace a future free from self-destructive behaviours, knowing that we are the architects of our transformation.

As you continue on your journey of letting go of self-destructive behaviours, remember that you possess the power to create positive change in your life. Embrace the lessons learned and the strategies gained, knowing that you are capable of living a life of balance, well-being, and personal fulfillment. Celebrate every milestone, no matter how small, and stay committed to sustaining your progress. You deserve a life filled with joy, growth, and positive change.

EMOTIONAL WOUNDS
and COPING STRATEGIES

Emotional wounds from abuse, traumas, addictions, toxic relationships and a negative past can have profound effects on our mental health. As we explore the depths of emotional wounds, we can face the immense challenges it presents. Emotional wounds have a profound impact on our lives, leaving indelible imprints on our hearts, minds, and spirits. Its effects can linger long after the initial event, casting a shadow over our sense of safety, well-being, and self-worth. Yet, within the darkest corners of our experiences, a glimmer of hope exists, a pathway toward healing and transformation.

In navigating emotional wounds, we can explore coping strategies that can guide us toward a place of healing, resilience, and renewal. We can venture into the intricacies of emotional pain, seeking to understand its multifaceted nature and how it shapes our lives. Through this understanding, we can lay the foundation for finding solace and reclaiming our inner strength.

Understanding the power to embrace imperfection marks the ups and downs, the triumphs and the setbacks. We can learn to navigate the recovery phases, each step propelling us closer to a renewed sense of self. Along the way, we can discover the power of grounding techniques, those simple yet profound practices that anchor us in the present moment and offer respite from the overwhelming weight of emotional wounds.

Healing goes beyond the mind; it encompasses the body, too. We can explore the vital connection between our physical and emotional well-being, venturing into the realm of somatic approaches to emotional wounds. By embracing the wisdom held within our bodies, we cultivate a harmonious relationship, allowing for profound restoration and a profound reconnection to ourselves.

Within the safety of a nurturing environment, we can create a sacred space for healing and processing. It is here that we find solace in the support of others, forging connections with individuals who understand the depths of our experiences. Building healthy relationships becomes a beacon of light, illuminating our path and reminding us that we are not alone.

In pursuing healing, we can encounter the profound need for self-care. Through the cultivation of personalized self-care rituals, we honour our physical, emotional, and mental well-being. We gift ourselves the compassion and tenderness we so rightfully deserve. As we develop these nourishing practices, we can discover the power they hold in replenishing our spirits and nurturing our souls.

Throughout this journey, we can find ourselves searching for meaning and purpose. We can embark on a quest to rediscover our values and aspirations, allowing them to guide us toward a newfound sense of direction. In the aftermath of emotional wounds, we unearth our resilience, channelling it into post-hurts that propel us forward and help us shape a life rich in meaning and purpose.

We can develop a firm belief that inner healing is possible. It may be an arduous path, filled with twists and turns, but within the darkness, there lies the potential for profound transformation. By embracing coping strategies and fostering a compassionate understanding of our experiences, we can open the door to a future where emotional wounds no longer define us. We must reclaim our strength, resilience, and joy along the way.

Emotional wounds have the power to profoundly impact our lives, shaping our experiences, perceptions, and sense of self. It is crucial to embark on a journey of understanding the intricate nature and how it affects us on multiple levels. By delving into this exploration, we gain insight into the diverse forms emotional wounds can take, such as physical, emotional, or psychological, and the unique ways they manifest in individuals.

Emotional wounds can stem from a range of sources, including childhood abuse, neglect, accidents, natural disasters, violence, and significant life-altering events. It permeates deep into the fabric of our being, influencing our thoughts, emotions, and behaviours. Recognizing and acknowledging the complexity of trauma empowers us to confront its effects head-on and initiate the healing process.

Moreover, emotional wounds can impact us uniquely, as each of us possesses vulnerabilities, coping mechanisms, and support systems. Some of us may struggle with flashbacks, nightmares, or hyperarousal, while others may experience dissociation, numbing, or a profound sense of loss. Understanding these variations allows us to approach recovery sensitively, recognizing that each person's journey is distinct and requires tailored support.

By exploring emotional wounds and their effects, we can

unravel the intricate web that weaves in our lives. We can better understand the triggers, emotional responses, and behavioural patterns that arise as a result. This understanding acts as a compass, guiding us toward effective coping strategies and healing modalities that address our unique needs and facilitate the process of recovery.

We need to reclaim our lives and rebuild our sense of self. It will grant us the necessary knowledge and insight to navigate the complexities of our experiences and embrace compassion for ourselves and others. We can then lay the foundation for a healing, resilience, and growth-filled future.

As we explore the path of healing from emotional wounds and embracing our imperfections, we can embark on a profound and transformative journey. This journey is not a straight and narrow road but rather a winding path that traverses through various recovery phases. Each phase holds its challenges, triumphs, and opportunities for growth.

At the beginning of our healing journey, we may feel overwhelmed by the weight of our past experiences. We may have been carrying the wounds deep within us, and the path ahead may seem daunting and uncertain. It is important to remember that healing is a process that takes time and patience to navigate its complexities.

We need to acknowledge the pain and the impact of emotional wounds. It is a time of facing our past head-on, embracing the problematic emotional pain that arises, and beginning to unravel the layers of hurt that have been buried within us. This phase may bring intense emotions, ranging from anger and sadness to fear and confusion. It is essential to allow ourselves to fully feel these emotions, honour our pain, and recognize that it is a necessary step towards healing.

As we move forward, we will enter a phase of exploration and self-discovery. We will seek resources, support, and guidance to assist us in our healing process. This may involve therapy, support groups, self-help books, or other modalities that resonate with us individually.

We can dig deep into our experiences, seeking to understand how emotional wounds have shaped us and identifying the patterns and triggers that have emerged as a result.

In the midst of this exploration, we can encounter moments of profound insight and self-reflection. We may start to recognize the ways in which emotional wounds have impacted our beliefs, relationships, and sense of self. We may question our worthiness, trust in others, and ability to experience joy and fulfilment. During these moments, we can begin to challenge and reshape our narratives, fostering self-compassion and cultivating a newfound sense of empowerment.

As the healing journey progresses, we gradually may shift into a phase of integration and growth. We must implement new coping strategies, cultivate resilience, and build a strong foundation for our emotional well-being. We must embrace self-care practices that nurture our physical, emotional, and spiritual selves. And develop a support network of trusted individuals who will uplift and inspire us along the way.

Ultimately, the healing journey will lead us to a place of renewed strength, authenticity, and purpose. We will discover hidden reservoirs of resilience within ourselves and tap into our inner wisdom. Our experiences of emotional wounds no longer define us but become a catalyst for personal growth and transformation. We can recognize that we are not defined by what has happened to us but by how we choose to heal and move forward.

Each individual's healing journey is unique, and there is no predetermined timeline or endpoint. It is a process of embracing our humanity, honouring our wounds, and finding the resilience to thrive despite the challenges we have faced. It requires courage, vulnerability, and a deep commitment to self-discovery and self-compassion.

As we explore the recovery phases, we can learn to trust in our resilience and embrace the possibility of a brighter future. The healing journey is not without its obstacles, but it is through facing these obstacles that we can uncover our true strength and reclaim our lives. We can embark on this transformative journey, supporting one another as we find our path to healing and reclaim our power.

One powerful tool that can aid in managing emotional hurts and promoting emotional stability is the practice of grounding techniques. When we experience emotional hurts, our minds and emotions can overwhelm us, leaving us unsettled. Grounding techniques offer a way to anchor ourselves in the present moment, providing stability and safety.

Mindfulness, a key component of grounding techniques, involves intentionally focusing on the present moment without judgment or attachment to the past or future. By bringing awareness to our immediate surroundings, sensations, and thoughts, we can shift our focus away from distressing memories or overwhelming emotions.

Practicing mindfulness can take many forms. It could be as simple as taking slow, deep breaths and observing the sensation of each breath entering and leaving our bodies. We can also engage our senses by paying attention to the sights, sounds, smells, tastes, and textures around us. By fully immersing ourselves in the present experience, we create a sense of grounding and connection to the here and now.

In addition to mindfulness, grounding exercises can be utilized to help us feel more anchored and centred. These exercises involve redirecting our attention to our physical body and the sensations it experiences. For example, we can focus on the feeling of our feet firmly planted on the ground, the pressure of our body against a chair or the floor, or the texture of an object held in our hands. By actively engaging with our physical sensations, we return to the present moment and establish a sense of stability and security.

Mindfulness, rooted in ancient contemplative traditions, has recently gained widespread recognition as a powerful tool for enhancing well-being and personal growth. Mindfulness practices can impact the very architecture of our brains. At its core, mindfulness is the art of paying attention to the present moment with non-judgmental awareness. It invites us to cultivate a deep self-awareness to observe our thoughts, emotions, and bodily sensations without clinging to or being carried away by them. By practicing mindfulness, we awaken to the richness of each moment and develop an intimate understanding of our mental and emotional processes.

Regular engagement in mindfulness meditation has been associated with changes in the structure and function of various brain regions involved in attention, emotion regulation, and self-awareness.

One of the key ways in which mindfulness promotes neural adaptation is through the cultivation of self-awareness. By consistently bringing our attention to the present moment, we develop a heightened sensitivity to our thoughts, emotions, and bodily sensations. This heightened self-awareness enables us to recognize patterns of thought and behaviours that may be detrimental to our well-being. With this awareness, we gain the opportunity to consciously choose how we respond to stimuli and break free from automatic, habitual reactions that no longer serve us.

Mindfulness also nurtures present-moment focus, which is vital for neural adaptation. In a world filled with distractions and constant stimulation, our attention often gets fragmented, pulling us away from the present and scattering our mental energy. However, through mindfulness practices, we train our minds to anchor themselves in the here and now. This focused attention strengthens the neural circuits associated with concentration and cognitive control, enabling us to navigate life's challenges with clarity and purpose.

Furthermore, mindfulness practices promote emotional regulation, another crucial aspect of neural adaptation. By developing a non-judgmental awareness of our emotions, we cultivate the capacity to observe them without being overwhelmed or reactive. This allows us to create space between our emotions and responses, allowing us to choose how we want to engage with our emotional experiences. Over time, this emotional regulation strengthens the neural networks involved in emotion processing, leading to increased emotional resilience and well-being.

Mindfulness techniques that facilitate neural adaptation include focused attention meditation, where we direct our attention to a specific object or sensation, and open monitoring meditation, where we cultivate a genuine awareness of our thoughts, emotions, and sensory experiences. These practices can be complemented by incorporating mindfulness into daily activities, such as mindful eating or walking, to bring a heightened sense of presence and awareness into our lives.

Furthermore, other practices, such as visualization or affirmations, can complement grounding techniques. Visualization involves creating a mental image of a safe and peaceful place or engaging in guided imagery exercises that promote relaxation and calmness. Conversely, affirmations involve repeating positive and empowering statements to ourselves, reinforcing our inner strength and resilience.

By incorporating grounding techniques into our daily lives, we can develop greater control over our emotions and reactions, even in the face of traumatic memories or triggers. These practices provide us with a solid foundation to navigate the challenges of emotional wounds, helping us find moments of peace, stability, and emotional well-being. As we continue on our healing journey, grounding techniques become valuable tools that support us in reclaiming our power and moving forward with renewed strength and resilience.

Recovering can be arduous, often filled with emotional challenges and setbacks. Developing emotional resilience as a solid foundation to navigate this difficult terrain and rebuild your life is crucial. Emotional resilience is the ability to bounce back from adversity, adapt to change, and thrive despite difficult circumstances. It empowers you to face the challenges of recovery with courage, strength, and determination.

Strengthening your emotional resilience begins with acknowledging and embracing your emotions as an integral part of your healing process. Understand that it's natural to experience various emotions, including anger, sadness, fear, and frustration. Give yourself permission to feel these emotions and express them in healthy ways.

Practice self-care to nurture your emotional well-being. Engage in activities that will bring you joy and promote relaxation. This could include spending time in nature, practicing mindfulness or meditation, journaling, or engaging in creative outlets like art or music. Cultivate a self-care routine that replenishes your emotional energy and provides moments of solace and rejuvenation.

Building emotional resilience also involves cultivating a positive mindset. Challenge negative self-talk and replace it with affirmations and empowering beliefs. Surround yourself with supportive and uplifting people who believe in your ability to heal and grow. Seek professional help, if needed, to explore deeper emotional wounds and develop effective coping strategies.

Additionally, embrace flexibility and adaptability as you navigate the ups and downs of emotional wound recovery. Recognize that setbacks are a normal part of the healing process and view them as opportunities for growth and learning. Embrace a growth mindset that believes in your capacity to overcome challenges and thrive despite adversity.

Remember, building emotional resilience takes time and patience. Be kind to yourself and celebrate small victories along the way. Each step you take towards strengthening your emotional resilience brings you closer to reclaiming your power and finding lasting healing.

As you continue on your journey of recovery, let the

development of emotional resilience be your guiding light, helping you overcome obstacles, cultivate inner strength, and emerge as a survivor who thrives in the face of adversity.

Cultivating self-care rituals can become an essential part of the healing process. It is about embracing the concept of self-nurturing and recognizing the importance of prioritizing one's well-being.

Cultivating self-care rituals involves developing personalized practices that cater to the unique needs of individuals. It goes beyond simple acts of pampering oneself; it encompasses a holistic approach to nurturing physical, emotional, and mental health. These rituals serve as intentional moments of self-reflection and self-compassion, allowing survivors to reconnect with their inner selves and foster a sense of inner peace.

Physical self-care rituals can range from regular exercise and nourishing the body with nutritious meals to relaxation techniques such as yoga or meditation. It can involve listening to the body's needs, recognizing boundaries, and establishing healthy habits that promote overall wellness.

Emotional self-care rituals involve creating a safe and supportive space to acknowledge and process emotions that may have been suppressed or neglected. This may include journaling, engaging in creative outlets, or seeking therapy or support groups where survivors can express their feelings and receive validation and understanding.

Mental self-care rituals focus on nurturing the mind and cultivating a positive mindset. This can involve engaging in activities that promote mental stimulation and growth, including reading, learning new skills, or practicing mindfulness exercises. It also includes setting boundaries around negative influences and engaging in self-talk that encourages self-compassion and self-belief.

Developing personalized self-care rituals is not a one-size-fits-all approach. It requires self-awareness and a willingness to explore different practices to find what resonates and brings a sense of inner balance and well-being. By investing time and energy in these rituals, survivors can gradually rebuild their sense of self, regain control over their lives, and create a solid foundation for long-term healing and empowerment.

Creating a safe space where you can find solace, support, and understanding is crucial. This safe space serves as a refuge, a sanctuary where the wounds can be tended to, and the healing process can unfold. It is a place where you can feel physically and emotionally secure as you navigate the difficult terrain of your negative experiences.

Creating a safe space begins with recognizing that healing requires a nurturing and non-judgmental environment. It involves surrounding yourself with people who offer empathy, compassion, and validation. These individuals can become pillars of support, lending a listening ear, a comforting presence, and a shoulder to lean on during moments of vulnerability.

In your safe space, it is essential to establish clear boundaries and guidelines that foster trust and respect. These boundaries ensure you feel safe expressing your emotions and experiences without fear of judgment or re-traumatization. It is a space where confidentiality is upheld, allowing individuals to speak their truth freely, knowing that their stories are held in the utmost confidence.

Creating a safe space involves cultivating an atmosphere of understanding and validation. It requires active listening, validating the emotions and experiences, and refraining from minimizing or dismissing pain. It is a space where your voice is heard and acknowledged, where you are encouraged to share your stories without fear of being silenced or invalidated.

Within this safe space, various healing modalities can be explored. Therapy, support groups, art therapy, mindfulness practices, or other forms of self-expression can all play a significant role in the healing journey. The safe space becomes a container for these healing practices, allowing you to explore your trauma, process your emotions, and discover new ways of coping and finding solace.

As the safe space is nurtured and maintained, you can gradually find the courage to face your traumas, confront your fears, and work towards healing and recovery. It becomes a haven of empowerment where you can reclaim your sense of agency and rebuild your shattered self-esteem. It is a space where resilience and growth can flourish as you gain strength from the supportive network that surrounds you.

Creating a safe space for healing and processing traumatic experiences is a transformative act of self-care and compassion. It is a commitment to prioritize your well-being and provide yourself with the nurturing environment needed for healing. With time, patience, and the unwavering support of those within the safe space, you can embark on a journey of healing, finding strength, and reclaiming your life in the aftermath.

Some of us may disconnect ourselves from our bodies, viewing them as a source of pain and vulnerability. The experiences we've endured may have left deep imprints on both our physical and emotional selves, causing us to feel detached, unsafe, or even betrayed by our bodies. However, healing from trauma requires us to reconnect with our bodies, reclaiming a sense of ownership and empowerment over this vessel that carries us through life.

Rebuilding a positive relationship with our bodies begins with gentle acknowledgment and acceptance of the physical sensations we experience. We need to learn to listen to the whispers and cries of our bodies, recognizing that they carry valuable messages and wisdom. Rather than suppressing or numbing these sensations, we need to learn to tune in and engage with them, honouring the intricate interconnectedness of our physical and emotional selves.

Somatic approaches offer us a pathway to healing by integrating the mind and body in the recovery process. Through somatic practices such as mindfulness, breathwork, gentle movement, and body-based therapies, we can release stored emotional pain, promote self-regulation, and foster a deep sense of safety within our bodies. These practices invite us to be present in the here and now, allowing us to observe and navigate our bodily sensations without judgment or fear.

In reconnecting with our bodies, we begin to cultivate self-compassion and nurture ourselves with kindness and gentleness. We need to learn to treat our bodies as allies rather than adversaries, understanding that they have carried us through the darkest of times and still have the capacity to heal and thrive. We can explore ways to engage in activities that promote self-care and bodily appreciation, including nourishing movement, body-centred therapies, and self-soothing practices.

As we traverse the path of reconnecting with our bodies, we may encounter resistance, discomfort, or triggers along the way. It is essential to approach this journey with patience and self-compassion, allowing ourselves the time and space needed for healing. Seeking the guidance and support of professionals, we can provide valuable insights and tailored techniques to facilitate our body's healing process.

Through the process of reconnecting with our bodies, we can begin to reclaim a sense of agency, trust, and empowerment. We can learn that our bodies are not mere vessels of pain but of resilience, strength, and transformation. By honouring and embracing our physical selves, we will unlock a profound source of healing, allowing us to navigate emotional wounds with a renewed sense of embodiment and wholeness.

Reclaiming personal strength, recovering from emotional wounds, and cultivating healthy relationships become vital to healing and growth. Nurturing supportive and nurturing connections with others provides a foundation of trust, empathy, and understanding that can profoundly impact our well-being.

We may have experienced broken trust, manipulation, and toxic dynamics in past relationships. Cultivating healthy relationships means intentionally seeking out individuals who respect and value us for who we are. It involves surrounding ourselves with people who uplift, encourage, and support our healing process.

To cultivate healthy relationships, it is crucial to establish clear boundaries that protect our emotional well-being. We can learn to recognize and assert our needs, communicate openly and honestly, and expect mutual respect from others. By setting boundaries, we can create a safe space where our emotions, vulnerabilities, and experiences are honoured and valued.

Building healthy relationships requires active listening and empathy. We can learn to truly hear and understand the perspectives and feelings of others, fostering deep connections and a sense of validation. Through empathy, we can create a compassionate environment where our own experiences are acknowledged and can extend understanding and support to those around us.

Nurturing healthy relationships involves a willingness to invest time and effort into building and maintaining connections. It means showing up for others and being present in their lives while also allowing them to reciprocate and be there for us. We seek relationships built on mutual trust, reciprocity, and shared values, creating a strong support network that promotes healing and growth.

We can find solace, encouragement, and inspiration in these healthy relationships. We can discover that we are not alone in our journey as we surround ourselves with individuals who understand our struggles and celebrate our victories. Together, we embark on a path of healing, learning, and personal transformation.

Cultivating healthy relationships is not without its challenges. It requires vulnerability and the willingness to let go of toxic connections that may hinder our progress. But as we prioritize our well-being and surround ourselves with positive influences, we can create a network of love and support that fosters our healing, encourages our growth, and reminds us of our inherent worth.

In the process of reclaiming power and rebuilding our lives, nurturing healthy relationships becomes a cornerstone of our journey. Through these connections, we can discover the strength, resilience, and joy that can arise when we cultivate bonds that nurture our souls and empower us to thrive.

Within the depths of emotional wounds lies a profound opportunity for personal growth and transformation. It is a journey in which we can navigate the complexities of healing, with the ultimate goal of becoming more assertive, wiser, and more resilient.

Emotional hurt is a concept that transcends mere survival. It invites us to embrace the challenges we have faced as catalysts for profound personal change. It is not a quick fix or a linear path but a courageous and introspective exploration of one's inner landscape.

Through the process of healing, we can come to understand the tremendous strength and resilience we possess. We can recognize the impact emotional wounds have had on our lives and the potential for growth within us. This transformative shift in perspective allows us to view our experiences as opportunities for learning, self-discovery, and profound personal evolution.

As we progress on our healing journey, we can notice subtle shifts in our thoughts, emotions, and outlook on life. We will develop a renewed appreciation for the simple joys and moments of connection. We will savour the present, understanding that we have emerged from the darkness and can now fully embrace the light.

Emotional wounds involve a deepening of empathy and compassion for oneself and others who have experienced similar journeys. We can learn to hold space for our pain and find solace in connecting with others who understand and validate our experiences.

Together, we can form a resilient community bound by our shared strength and determination.

In the midst of emotional wounds, we can re-evaluate our priorities and values. We can gain clarity on what truly matters to us and make intentional choices aligned with our newfound understanding. We may pursue passions we once believed were unattainable or become advocates for change, using our experiences to bring about positive transformations in our own lives and the lives of others.

The path of emotional wounds is not without challenges. There will be setbacks, moments of doubt, and days when the weight of the past feels overwhelming. However, through these very struggles, we can discover our resilience and courage. We can rise above adversity, find strength in vulnerability and continue to move forward despite obstacles.

Emotional wounds are a testament to the indomitable human spirit. It is a narrative of hope, resilience, and the enduring power of the human soul to overcome even the most devastating experiences. It serves as a reminder that healing is not only possible but can lead to profound personal transformation.

Within emotional wounds, intricate layers are waiting to be unravelled, offering us practical guidance and coping strategies to aid us in our journey of healing and transformation. It is a landscape adorned with resilience, courage, and the unyielding human spirit.

As we embark on our path of emotional wounds, we may encounter a myriad of challenges and emotions. It is a process that requires gentle self-exploration, patience, and a willingness to face the remnants of our past. As we focus on the depths of our emotional scars, we will peel back layers of pain and vulnerability while holding onto the flicker of hope that lies within.

Guidance on this transformative journey is multifaceted. It begins with recognizing that healing is not a linear process but a nonlinear dance between progress and setbacks. We will learn to embrace the ebb and flow of our emotions, allowing ourselves to grieve, feel anger, and find solace in moments of peace.

Coping strategies become our trusted companions, offering support and stability in the face of adversity. Mindfulness and grounding techniques provide anchors in times of distress, helping survivors navigate the overwhelming waves of emotion. Through these practices, we can learn to reconnect with the present moment, anchoring ourselves in the here and now.

Self-care rituals become a sacred act of self-nurturing as we discover the power of caring for our physical, emotional, and mental well-being. We create personalized practices that replenish our energy, whether it be through gentle exercise, journaling, or immersing ourselves in nature's embrace. These rituals become beacons of self-compassion, reminding us that we deserve love and care.

The support of others plays a vital role in the journey of emotional wounds. We seek connections with individuals who can hold space for our experiences, providing a safe haven where we can share our stories without judgment. We may engage in support group therapy sessions or cultivate relationships with loved ones who offer unwavering support and understanding.

As we progress, we cultivate a newfound sense of purpose and meaning. We seek opportunities for personal growth and learning, transforming our emotional wounds into a catalyst for positive change. This may involve engaging in advocacy work, sharing our experiences to raise awareness, or finding solace in creative outlets that allow us to express ourselves authentically.

The intricacies of emotional wounds lie in the delicate balance between self-reflection and forward movement. We can learn to honour our past while embracing the possibilities of our future. We can navigate the complexities of forgiveness for ourselves and those who have caused us harm. We redefine our identity, no longer defined solely by our emotional pain but by the strength, resilience, and wisdom we have cultivated along our journey. Ultimately, emotional wounds offer us an opportunity to survive and thrive.

As we conclude this chapter on emotional wounds and coping strategies, we reflect upon the immense resilience and strength of individuals who have endured. Throughout this transformative journey, we have deepened our understanding of emotional wounds and their profound effects on individual lives. We have embarked on a healing path, navigating the phases of emotional pain and finding our unique paths to healing.

Grounding techniques have become valuable tools in managing emotional wounds and promoting emotional stability. We have embraced mindfulness and grounding exercises, anchoring ourselves in the present moment and fostering a sense of safety and stability.

Building emotional resilience has been an essential aspect of our journey. We have recognized our capacity to adapt and overcome the challenges of emotional wound recovery. We have cultivated emotional strength through various practices and strategies, allowing us to face adversity with courage and determination.

Self-care rituals have played a significant role in our healing process. We have prioritized our physical, emotional, and mental well-being, developing personalized practices that nurture and restore us. By honouring our needs, we have replenished our inner resources and fostered a foundation of self-compassion and care.

Creating a safe space has been vital in our healing journey. We have surrounded ourselves with support and established environments that promote healing, growth, and understanding. Within these spaces, we have been able to process and integrate our traumatic experiences, finding solace and connection along the way.

Reconnecting with our bodies has been a transformative step in our healing process. We have rebuilt a positive relationship with our bodies, acknowledging their wisdom and resilience. Exploring somatic approaches to emotional healing, we have discovered new avenues for healing and releasing emotional wounds from within.

Amidst the challenges of emotional wounds, we have sought meaning and purpose. We have delved into the depths of our experiences, searching for insight and understanding. In this search, we have reconnected with our values and aspirations, finding inspiration and direction for our lives beyond the emotional wounds.

Nurturing healthy relationships has been an invaluable source of support and growth. We have cultivated connections with individuals who understand, validate, and uplift us on our healing journey. These relationships have become pillars of strength, providing comfort, encouragement, and a sense of belonging.

As we conclude this chapter, we do so with hope and optimism. We recognize the potential for personal growth and transformation from healing wounds. Emotional wounds have become a beacon of possibility, reminding us of our inherent capacity to rise above adversity and create a life filled with meaning and purpose.

As you continue on your healing path, know that you are not alone. You possess immense strength and resilience within you. Embrace the coping strategies and insights you have gained, and may they guide you toward a life of healing and growth. You can transform your pain into purpose, and as you navigate this journey, may you find solace, support, and a renewed sense of hope.

FAILURE *as*
FERTILIZERS

Failure is an inevitable part of life, yet it is often met with fear, disappointment, and self-doubt. However, by shifting our perspective and embracing failure as a stepping stone to success, we can unlock a wealth of personal growth, resilience, and invaluable lessons. We need to condition the mind and develop a culture of this form of understanding.

One of the first steps in embracing failure is redefining our understanding. Instead of viewing failure as an outcome or a reflection of our worth, we can reframe it as a temporary setback, an opportunity to learn, and a necessary step toward success. Failure can become a valuable teacher, offering insights into our strengths, weaknesses, and areas for improvement.

Failure provides us with an opportunity for introspection and self-reflection. It encourages us to evaluate our strategies, actions, and mindset, enabling us to identify what worked and what didn't.

Examining our failures with curiosity and an open mind can extract valuable lessons that contribute to our personal and professional growth.

Moreover, failure builds resilience and mental fortitude. When we experience setbacks, we face challenges that test our perseverance and determination. By embracing failure, we develop the resilience to bounce back, adapt, and progress despite obstacles. Each failure becomes a stepping stone that strengthens our resolve and equips us with the tenacity needed to overcome future hurdles.

In pursuing success, failure becomes an integral part of the process. History is adorned with stories of individuals who encountered numerous failures before achieving remarkable success. Thomas Edison, the light bulb inventor, famously said, "I have not failed. I've just found 10,000 ways that won't work." These luminaries embraced failure as an essential ingredient in their journey toward greatness, using it as fuel to persist and innovate.

To fully embrace failure, it is important to adopt a growth mindset. A growth mindset recognizes that abilities and skills can be developed through dedication, effort, and learning from mistakes. When we approach failure with a growth mindset, we view it as an opportunity for growth and expansion rather than a reflection of our limitations. We understand that failure does not define us but instead allows us to improve and evolve.

Furthermore, surrounding ourselves with a supportive network of individuals with similar mindsets can significantly impact our ability to embrace failure. Connecting with like-minded people who understand the value of failure as a stepping stone to success can provide encouragement, guidance, and a sense of camaraderie. By sharing our failures and learning from the experiences of others, we create a supportive ecosystem that fosters growth and resilience.

We must condition our minds to understand that failure is a powerful tool that can significantly impact our mindset, emotional well-being, and overall outlook. It involves consciously choosing uplifting and affirming words and thoughts to counteract self-doubt, negative beliefs, and self-criticism. We can foster self-confidence, resilience, and a deep sense of self-worth by cultivating a supportive inner dialogue. Let's explore some effective techniques for practicing positive self-talk.

One fundamental aspect of failure is becoming aware of our internal dialogue. Often, we engage in automatic negative thinking patterns without even realizing it. We can identify negative or self-defeating patterns by paying attention to our thoughts and the language we use to describe ourselves and our experiences. Awareness is the first step towards change, where we use failure as fertilizers.

Once we become aware of failure, we can challenge and reframe what they are. This involves consciously replacing negative or limiting beliefs with positive and empowering ones. For example, if we catch ourselves saying, "I'm not good enough," we can reframe it as "I am capable and deserving of success." By reframing our thoughts in a more positive light, we shift our perspective and empower ourselves.

Failure encourages us to practice positive self-talk. Affirmations are positive statements we repeat to ourselves regularly, silently or aloud. They are designed to reinforce positive beliefs and encourage a more optimistic mindset. Examples of affirmations include statements such as, "I am confident and capable," "I embrace challenges as opportunities for growth," or "I am deserving of love and happiness." By consistently affirming these positive statements, we gradually "Embrace Imperfections" and internalize empowering beliefs.

It's essential to choose affirmations that resonate with us. We can reflect on areas where we want to experience more positivity, such as relationships, careers, or self-image. Tailoring affirmations to specific focus areas allows us to address our unique needs and aspirations. Writing affirmations down and placing them in visible locations, such as on a mirror or computer screen, serves as a reminder to practice positive self-talk throughout the day.

In addition to affirmations, practicing self-compassion is crucial in cultivating positive self-talk. It involves treating ourselves with kindness and understanding, especially during challenging times or when we make mistakes. Instead of berating ourselves for perceived shortcomings, we can offer encouragement and support. For instance, if we encounter a setback, we can remind ourselves, "It's okay to make mistakes; they are opportunities for growth. I am learning and improving every day."

Consistency is key when practicing positive self-talk. Like any habit, it takes time and effort to develop. It's essential to be patient and persistent, understanding that transformation occurs gradually. By integrating positive self-talk into our daily routines and making it a priority, we reinforce the practice and embed it in our subconscious mind.

Letting go of failure and embracing forgiveness is a profound and transformative process that can liberate us from the burdens of negative emotions and promote inner healing. Holding onto failures, including resentments, grievances, or grudges, not only weighs heavily on our minds and hearts but also restricts our ability to experience genuine happiness and build healthy relationships.

When we harbour failure, we allow negative emotions to consume us, keeping us trapped in a cycle of bitterness and anger. It drains our energy and prevents us from fully embracing the present moment and moving forward. However, by consciously choosing to let go and forgive, we reclaim our power and create space for healing and growth.

Failure is not about condoning or forgetting the harm they may have caused. It is a personal decision to release ourselves from the emotional shackles that bind us. It is a conscious choice to prioritize our well-being over holding onto the pain of the past. By forgiving, we untether ourselves from the negative influence of those who have wronged us, allowing us to move forward with greater clarity, peace, and compassion.

Failure is a journey that begins with understanding and empathy, which we discussed earlier. It involves recognizing the humanity in others and acknowledging that everyone is capable of making mistakes. It does not mean that we must justify or excuse the actions of others, but rather, it is an act of choosing compassion over resentment.

To embark on the path of failure, reflecting on our own experiences of making mistakes and seeking forgiveness from others can be helpful. Recognizing our fallibility allows us to empathize with the imperfections of others, fostering a sense of compassion and understanding.

Additionally, failure requires a willingness to let go of the desire for revenge or retribution. It means relinquishing the belief that holding onto anger will bring us justice or satisfaction. Instead, failure allows us to break free from the cycle of negativity and create space for healing and personal growth.

Practicing forgiveness also involves self-compassion. Sometimes, we hold onto failure towards ourselves for past mistakes or perceived shortcomings. Learning to forgive ourselves is an essential aspect of the healing process. By embracing self-forgiveness, we cultivate self-love and acceptance, allowing us to move forward with a renewed sense of purpose and positivity.

It is important to note that letting go of failure is a profoundly personal journey, and it may take time and effort to fully let go of past resentments. It is a process that requires self-reflection, introspection, and sometimes seeking support from trusted friends, family, or professionals.

In the end, letting go is an act of self-empowerment. It enables us to reclaim control over our emotions, release the burden of negative energy, and create space for joy, peace, and personal growth. By embracing failure, we open ourselves to a future filled with greater compassion, understanding, and the potential for deeper connections with others.

INNER HEALING

In the realm of embracing imperfections, trust forms the cornerstone of a strong and lasting bond. It's an invisible thread that weaves together hearts and souls, providing a sense of security and emotional connection. But when support for abuse, traumas, regrets, wrongdoing, broken toxic relationships and other emotional wounds are shattered, the very foundation of inner healing crumbles beneath our feet. Emotional wounds have a profound impact on our lives, leaving indelible imprints on our hearts, minds, and spirits. The pain is deep, the wounds are raw, and the road to inner healing seems treacherous and uncertain. Inner healing from emotional wounds and our imperfections is a journey that requires courage, vulnerability, and a commitment to growth. We need to face the intricate nuances of rebuilding and reconnecting on an emotional level.

The emotional aftermath of emotional brokenness is nothing short of a rollercoaster ride. The torrent of emotions, from anger to sadness and confusion, can leave us feeling lost in a sea of uncertainty. But within the depths of despair lies the potential for inner healing. We unravel the intricacies of rebuilding, piece by piece, with delicate care and patience. We navigate the labyrinth of emotions, providing guidance and strategies to foster effective communication and facilitate the process of inner healing. Exploring the terrain of self-reflection, self-care, and the path toward forgiveness is necessary to move from emotional wounds to inner healing. It's the only way we can Embrace Imperfection.

It's important to note that inner healing from emotional wounds and facing our imperfections is a highly personal journey unique to each individual and relationship. There is no one-size-fits-all approach, no magic formula that instantly mends the broken pieces. We need tools, insights, and stories of resilience that may empower us on our path to inner healing.

Whether you find yourself in the aftermath of emotional wounds or wish to support a loved one through this tumultuous terrain, it is a testament to the strength of the human spirit and the enduring capacity for love and forgiveness. It is a journey of inner healing, rebuilding trust, and rediscovering the resilience within us.

Understanding the intricate web of emotions that weaves its way through our hearts and minds is essential. Emotional wounds strike at the core of our being, shaking our sense of security and leaving us bewildered amidst a whirlwind of emotions. This is where inner healing begins to bring us back to the pathway of happiness.

Inner Healing can be like an emotional rollercoaster that follows the revelation of betrayal. It begins with shock, that sudden jolt that rocks your very foundation. Your mind races, desperately trying to comprehend what has just been revealed. Denial may take hold, a protective shield that tries to shield you from the painful truth from the depths of the emotional wounds. But as denial fades, waves of anger crash over you like a furious storm, the fire of emotional pain burning deep within.

Sadness embraces you next, wrapping you in its cold arms, embrace as you mourn the loss of what happened and the negative outcome you feel, shattering your heart with unbearable emotional pain. Questions flood your mind: Why did this happen? What did I do wrong? Why did I do that? Why did I say yes? Why was I forced into doing something I did not agree to do? Why didn't I do this, that or the other? Doubt clouds your judgment, eroding your self-esteem and leaving you questioning your worth.

Mixed in with the torrent of emotions, there may be moments of confusion. How can you possibly make sense of something incomprehensible? You may find yourself oscillating between love and hate, forgiveness and resentment. It's a tangled web of conflicting emotions, pulling you in different directions. Yet, amidst the chaos, there is a glimmer of hope—a beacon that signals the beginning of inner healing. In the depths of despair, we find the strength to confront our emotions head-on, to examine them with an open heart and a curious mind. By understanding the emotional impact, we can begin to untangle the threads that bind us to pain and chart a course toward inner healing.

Our emotions are valid and worthy of acknowledgment. Through understanding and embracing these emotions, we can embark on a transformative journey of inner healing. We must discover the strength to rise above the pain and rebuild what has been broken.

Trust, like fragile porcelain, can be shattered with a single act; trusting ourselves and others leaves us exposed and vulnerable. However, within the realm of vulnerability lies the opportunity for profound growth and connection. Restoring our regrets or taking control of our lives is not a journey to be taken lightly. It requires patience, commitment, and unwavering dedication. It's a process that unfolds gradually, akin to mending a tapestry thread by thread, weaving together the fabric of inner healing from what has been torn apart.

The transformative path should be open and honest communication with ourselves. It is through heartfelt conversations that the deep wounds can be explored and understood. There must be a time to express feelings, fears, and hopes—listening with empathy and compassion, seeking to comprehend the intricate layers of pain.

As the delicate threads of communication strengthen, establishing clear boundaries and limitations are established to prevent or avoid the emotional wound from occurring. These boundaries serve as protective shields, offering reassurance and accountability. They provide a sense of safety, allowing inner healing to start.

In the realm of inner healing, actions speak louder than words. Consistency and reliability become the building blocks of restoration. Promises must be accompanied by unwavering commitment, where deeds align with words. Trust takes root when actions consistently demonstrate reliability, honesty, and integrity.

Acknowledging that inner healing from emotional wounds and our imperfections is not a solo endeavour is crucial. Seeking professional help can provide invaluable guidance and support along the way. A trained therapist can offer tools and techniques tailored to your unique circumstances, facilitating open dialogue and fostering more profound understanding.

As discussed earlier, self-care and self-reflection are vital components of the trust restoration journey. We need to nurture ourselves, to heal our wounds, and to reflect upon the factors that led to emotional wounds. Self-reflection allows for growth and personal development, encouraging us to explore our vulnerabilities, triggers, and patterns.

Ultimately, rebuilding is a testament to the enduring strength of love and the human spirit. It requires courage, vulnerability, and a shared commitment to growth. It's a journey that unfolds gradually, sometimes with setbacks and moments of doubt. Yet, as you embark on this path, you must hold onto the belief that you can rebuild yourself and that love can rise from the ashes more robust than ever. Take heart and gather your strength. Embrace the challenges, the tears, and the triumphs that lie ahead. As you navigate the intricate terrain of rebuilding your life, you need to remember that inner healing is possible, and the power of love and resilience knows no bounds.

Building a bridge that spans the chasm of hurt is one of the most vital tools in inner healing. This opens the conversation, allowing us to rebuild emotional connections and forge a stronger bond.

Visual yourself sitting across from your predator, the weight of unspoken words hanging heavy in the air. Your hearts ache with longing for understanding and connection, yet the fear of judgment and further pain threatens to silence your voices. It's in moments like these that the power of effective communication truly shines.

Navigating difficult conversations is a delicate dance requiring vulnerability, active listening, and empathy. It's about creating a safe space to express your feelings, fears, and desires without fear of condemnation or dismissal. It's about embracing uncomfortable truths and exploring the complexities of emotions that arise.

But how do you begin? How do you find the words to articulate the depths of your pain or your longing to be healed? It starts with setting the stage, a foundation of trust and openness that allows you to feel safe expressing your emotions.

In these conversations, practicing being a speaker and an active listener is essential. You need to truly hear what is spoken from the depths of your heart, the wounds, without interruption or judgment. It's about learning to be a speaker and listener without interruption. It's about acknowledging your pain, validating your emotions, and showing genuine empathy. Remember, your feelings are valid, even if they challenge your perspective.

Moreover, effective communication involves owning your part in the situation, taking responsibility for your actions, expressing remorse, and demonstrating a genuine willingness to change. This openness fosters an environment where inner healing and growth can thrive.

It's important to be mindful of the power of language. Choose your words carefully, for they hold the potential to heal or wound. Speak from a place of compassion and kindness, aiming to understand and be understood. Embrace the vulnerability required to share your deepest emotions.

Rebuilding your emotional life is not a linear process. It requires patience, time, and a commitment to the inner healing process step by step. Difficult conversations may be met with resistance, tears, or moments of silence. But in those moments, remain steadfast and resilient, for they are opportunities for growth and understanding.

As we embark on this journey of inner healing and rebuilding, let us embrace the transformative power of effective communication. Let us listen with open hearts, speak with intention, and foster an environment of love, understanding, and growth. Together, we can navigate these challenging conversations and reconnect on a deeper level, paving the way for a future built on trust, empathy, and genuine emotional connection. This helps us embrace imperfection from the hurt without letting it stay painful.

As we delve into the depths of inner healing, we will come face to face with a tumultuous storm of emotions. Like crashing waves against the shore, the pain can feel overwhelming, engulfing our very being. During these moments of anguish, we must find solace in the art of processing and expressing our pain.

It is perfectly natural to feel a whirlwind of emotions when emotionally hurt. Anger may surge through your veins, fueled by a sense of betrayal. Sadness may cast a shadow upon your heart, leaving you feeling lost and broken. Confusion may cloud your mind as you grapple with the complexities of the situation.

In the midst of this emotional storm, it is crucial to grant yourself permission to feel. Suppressing or denying these intense emotions will only prolong the inner healing process. Instead, let the tears flow, allow the anger to rise and fall like a tempest, and surrender to the rawness of your pain. Allow your mind to remember there is a cause for everything in life: every action, behaviour and choice.

But expression alone is not enough; the act of processing must accompany it. Through this process, we begin to make sense of our emotions, unravelling the tangled threads of hurt and seeking clarity amidst the chaos. We need to find solace in the act of self-reflection. Take time to pause, to retreat into the sanctuary of your thoughts, and to explore the depths of your emotions. Ask yourself difficult questions. What triggers these intense feelings? How do your weaknesses challenge your sense of self-worth and trust? What expectations and beliefs are shattered by emotional wounds?

As you navigate these internal landscapes, remember to practice self-compassion. Be gentle with yourself, for the pain you carry is heavy. Offer yourself the kindness and understanding that you would extend to a dear friend in need. Allow yourself the space to heal at your own pace, knowing that inner healing is not linear but a journey of peaks and valleys.

Remember, processing and expressing your pain is vital to your inner healing journey. It is through this courageous act that you reclaim your voice, honour your emotions, and begin to forge a path toward inner peace. Though the road may be arduous, you possess an innate strength to weather the storm and emerge on the other side transformed and resilient.

Embrace the power of processing and expressing your pain. Let it wash over you, acknowledge its presence, and channel its energy towards your inner healing. Through this process, you will find the seeds of growth and renewal amidst the wreckage, moving closer to the light that awaits beyond the shadows of how you feel and the emotional wound you carry.

Boundaries serve as the protective walls that safeguard our emotional well-being, while relationship agreements create a solid foundation of trust and accountability.

Trust is shattered in the wake of emotional wounds, leaving us feeling vulnerable and uncertain. It's in this delicate phase that boundaries take on even greater significance. They provide a sense of safety, allowing us to heal and rebuild at our own pace. By clearly defining what is acceptable and what is not, we set the framework for rebuilding trust and protecting ourselves from further harm.

Establishing boundaries and settling limitations is an act of self-care, a declaration of our worth and needs. It may involve setting limits on specific behaviours or establishing guidelines for communication and transparency. Boundaries empower us to voice our expectations and ensure our emotional well-being remains a priority.

In addition to boundaries, taking control back for our lives, a shared understanding and framework for rebuilding happiness. They foster being real, endure open and honest communication with ourselves and put closure to the hurt. We will come to a place where we realize we cannot change the past; we cannot "fix" a person or change them, but we can change ourselves and how we think. We can make wiser decisions to be healed and stay healed.

Creating these agreements requires open dialogue, vulnerability, and a willingness to rebuild from the hurt. It is a collaborative effort where we define the terms that will guide our journey of inner healing. Remember, these agreements are not meant to restrict or control but to create a supportive environment where inner healing can be nurtured.

Boundaries may evolve over time as inner healing progresses and life is rebuilt. Flexibility and ongoing communication are vital in ensuring these agreements meet the changing needs.

The process of relationship repair and rebuilding can be a difficult challenge. Like a fragile flower pushing through cracks in concrete, love has the remarkable ability to find a way to flourish even after the darkest storms.

After the storm of emotional hurts has passed, the road to rebuilding may appear daunting, strewn with doubts and uncertainties. You may question whether the healthy you will ever be resurrected and the emotional bond can be fortified once again. But with dedication, open communication, and a shared commitment to growth, the journey of repair is possible.

It begins with an honest acknowledgment of the pain and the courage to face the wounds head-on. You must be willing to engage in heartfelt conversations, gently peeling back the layers of hurt and expressing your emotions with vulnerability. Active listening and empathy play pivotal roles in this sacred space, allowing you to feel seen, heard, and understood.

Through this open dialogue, the process of rebuilding can take root. Inner healing does not come overnight; it requires consistent actions and transparent behaviour. It necessitates patience, as the emotional wounds and negative thoughts are addressed by ourselves, taking baby steps towards healing. We need to believe in the possibility of a renewed emotional connection. Trust is a delicate dance, one step forward and occasionally two steps back, but with each genuine effort, the foundation grows stronger.

Love, hope, trust, confidence, self-esteem, and self-security must be rekindled amidst the inner healing process, starting with small baby steps or a lingering gaze that reawakens the connection that once thrived. Although it may have been damaged, communication can be rebuilt over time through patience, understanding, and a shared commitment to vulnerability. Rebuilding extends beyond the physical realm.

Emotional healing, the deep connection that binds hearts and souls, requires nurturing and intentional effort. It involves the willingness to be open to sharing fears, dreams, and vulnerabilities. The seeds of hope can be planted by cultivating a safe space for expressing beliefs and feelings.

Inner healing and rebuilding take time. Patience and self-compassion are your allies as you navigate the intricate terrain of repairing what was once broken. It is a journey that may test your beliefs, but it is also an opportunity for growth, resilience, and a deeper understanding of the complexities of love.

While the path may be challenging, the rewards of repair and the rekindling of a happy life are immeasurable. With each step forward, with each tender act of forgiveness and understanding, you draw closer to the possibility of a love that transcends the wounds of the past. Embrace the journey, embrace the growth, and let the process of inner healing guide you toward restoring a stronger and more resilient bond than ever before.

As you navigate the turbulent waters of healing, it is crucial to remember one person who often gets neglected in the process is yourself. Amidst the chaos of emotions and the effort to rebuild trust, self-care becomes an anchor—a sanctuary where you can find solace and strength.

Imagine a quiet corner where you can retreat, allowing yourself the space and time to process your feelings and reflect on your journey. This is where self-care and self-reflection come into play. It's about embracing moments of stillness and introspection, where you prioritize your well-being and embark on a profound journey of self-discovery.

Self-care is not selfish; it's an act of self-preservation and self-love. It is about recognizing your needs and taking deliberate steps to meet them. It may involve engaging in activities that bring you joy and peace, including practicing yoga, taking long walks in nature, indulging in a soothing bubble bath, or losing yourself in the pages of a captivating book. It could also mean seeking support from trusted friends or professionals who can provide guidance and lend a compassionate ear.

Self-reflection, on the other hand, is a powerful tool for growth and transformation. It's an invitation to delve deep into the recesses of your being, examining your values, desires, and aspirations. It's a chance to confront your vulnerabilities, acknowledge your strengths, and cultivate a deeper understanding of yourself.

During the inner healing process, self-reflection offers a pathway to make sense of the tangled emotions and complex dynamics that arise. It allows you to gain insights into your role in the relationship and uncover patterns that may have contributed to your emotional wounds or the imperfections you see in yourself. Through this introspection, you can develop a heightened self-awareness, paving the way for personal growth and change.

Prioritizing self-care and self-reflection is not always easy. It requires carving out dedicated time in your busy life, setting boundaries, and honouring your needs. It may involve making difficult decisions that serve your well-being, even if they initially seem daunting.

Remember that inner healing is not just about rebuilding trust— it's also about reclaiming your sense of self and finding inner peace. By engaging in self-care practices and embracing self-reflection, you embark on a transformative journey of self-discovery. You have the power to emerge from this experience more robust, wiser, and more resilient.

Take a deep breath and listen to the whispers of your heart. Allow self-care and self-reflection to be your guiding compass as you navigate the path toward healing. Embrace the profound opportunity to nurture yourself, to rediscover your worth, and to emerge as a more whole and authentic version of yourself.

You are deserving of love, compassion, and growth. Embrace this journey of self-care and self-reflection, and may it lead you towards a brighter and more empowered future.

Imagine standing at a crossroads, uncertain of which path to take. Doubt clouds your mind, and you find yourself questioning your judgment and instincts. The once unshakeable confidence within you feels fragile, tarnished by past experiences and moments of self-doubt. It's a place many of us have found ourselves in, and it's a place from which we can emerge more substantial and more self-assured.

Inner healing is an essential step toward personal growth and empowerment. It's a journey that requires introspection, compassion, and a commitment to cultivating a renewed sense of confidence in your abilities.

To rebuild yourself, you must first acknowledge the moments and experiences that eroded it. It may have been a series of decisions that didn't align with your values or instincts, or perhaps the pain of betrayal shattered your belief in your judgment. Whatever the cause, it's time to face it head-on with unwavering honesty.

Through introspection and self-reflection, we have an opportunity to gain deeper insights into our past choices and actions. It's not about dwelling in regret or self-blame but rather about understanding the circumstances, motivations, and underlying beliefs that influenced our decisions. By embracing this understanding, we can begin to untangle the threads of self-doubt and reconstruct a solid foundation of self-trust.

Engaging in self-reflection is a pivotal practice that empowers us to gain profound insight into the underlying motivations behind our healing. It serves as a powerful tool for unravelling the intricate layers of our thoughts, emotions, and experiences, enabling us to understand ourselves on a deeper level.

One of the primary methods of inner healing is journaling, where we set aside dedicated time to express our thoughts and feelings on paper. Through the act of writing, we create a safe space for self-expression, free from judgment or external influence. As we pour our innermost thoughts onto the pages, patterns emerge, revealing recurring triggers and the emotions fueling our impulsive actions.

Within the sacred pages of our journals, we can explore the origins of our emotional wounds. We might find that certain events or past traumas have left lasting imprints, influencing our responses and decision-making processes. By examining these experiences, we gain a deeper understanding of how they continue to shape our present actions.

Introspection is a powerful form of self-reflection that involves delving inward and deep contemplation. It calls for moments of quiet solitude, where we intentionally turn our attention inward and examine our thoughts, beliefs, and desires. Through introspection, we uncover the subtle whispers of our inner voice, revealing the true desires and needs that drive our emotional wounds.

During the process of self-reflection, we may encounter uncomfortable truths or conflicting emotions. It is important to approach this practice with gentleness and self-compassion as we navigate the complexities of our inner landscape. By cultivating a non-judgmental attitude, we create a safe and nurturing environment for self-exploration, allowing for honest and transformative discoveries.

Through healing, we can uncover the multifaceted layers of our emotional wounds. We will recognize the deep-seated fears, insecurities, or unmet needs that manifest themselves. It sheds light on the underlying motivations that often remain hidden beneath the surface, providing us with a clearer understanding of ourselves and our healing patterns.

As we gain insights through our focus on inner healing, we can become better equipped to address the root causes of our emotional wounds. Armed with this knowledge, we can develop targeted strategies and coping mechanisms to counteract issues from reoccurring. By consciously redirecting our thoughts and actions, we can take ownership of our lives, breaking free from the cycle of being wounded emotionally.

Inner healing is not a one-time endeavour but rather an ongoing practice. Our motivations and triggers may change as we evolve and grow, necessitating continuous exploration and self-awareness. By incorporating self-reflection into our daily lives, we can foster a deeper connection with ourselves and lay the groundwork for sustained personal transformation.

Restoring self-trust will occur, which involves extending compassion and forgiveness to ourselves. We all make mistakes; we are beautifully imperfect beings navigating a complex world. It's crucial to acknowledge that growth and learning emerge from these moments of imperfection. By embracing self-compassion, we release the heavy burden of self-judgment and create space for growth and transformation.

One of the critical elements in inner healing is learning to listen to our intuition, the whispers of wisdom that reside within us. Intuition is that inner compass that guides us towards what feels right and authentic. Cultivating a connection with our intuition involves slowing down, quieting the noise around us, and truly tuning in to the subtle signals our inner voice sends. Trusting our intuition is a powerful step towards reclaiming our confidence and belief in our judgment.

Inner healing is not an overnight process. It requires patience, resilience, and a willingness to embrace vulnerability. Within you lies an infinite well of strength and wisdom. You have the power to rediscover your inner knowing, make choices aligned with your values, and step forward confidently into the bright horizon of your future.

Breathe profoundly and anchor yourself in the belief that you are worthy of your trust. Embrace this opportunity to rebuild, grow, and step forward with a newfound confidence in your judgment and instincts. The road may be winding, but with each step, you will rediscover the unwavering power that resides within you. Trust yourself, and the world will trust you too.

As you tread the path of healing, you may find yourself standing at a crossroads. The choices before you are both challenging and empowering. Within this pivotal moment, you have the power to shape your future, determine the course of your relationships, and nurture the growth that lies dormant within.

Moving forward requires courage to face the truth, confront the pain head-on, and embrace the possibility of a renewed sense of trust and connection. It is a process that demands vulnerability as you allow yourself to be open to the possibility of inner healing and rebuilding what was once shattered. It won't be easy; there may be setbacks along the way, moments of doubt and uncertainty. But remember, the journey toward trust and connection is gradual, a delicate dance of patience and perseverance.

Embracing a renewed sense of trust and connection entails nurturing the seeds of forgiveness for yourself and those who hurt you. It means engaging in heartfelt conversations, allowing emotions to be expressed and heard, and working together to rebuild the emotional bond that was ruptured. It's about embracing vulnerability and allowing yourself to be seen and known, scars and all. It's a process that requires consistent effort, understanding, and a willingness to learn and grow together.

As you navigate the terrain of inner healing, it is essential to acknowledge that the path may also lead you toward separation and growth. There are instances when inner healing comes not only in the form of restoration but through the process of letting go. Sometimes, the wounds run too deep, and the broken pieces cannot be reassembled similarly. In these moments, it takes tremendous strength to honour your well-being and chart a new life course.

Navigating separation and growth requires an introspective journey, a deep dive into understanding your needs, desires, and boundaries. It's about rediscovering your strength and embracing the possibilities that lie beyond the confines of the relationship. It may involve seeking support through therapy, counselling, or the comforting presence of loved ones who stand by your side. It's about finding solace in the knowledge that growth and transformation can emerge from the most painful experiences.

The path forward is not a linear one. It twists and turns, filled with both triumphs and setbacks. But with each step you take, you are reclaiming your power, embracing your resilience, and creating a future anchored in self-discovery, growth, and the pursuit of genuine happiness. The choice is yours.

Sometimes, the wounds inflicted by emotional wounds can run deep, leaving us grappling with a whirlwind of emotional scars and questions that seem impossible to answer. In these moments, seeking professional help can be a guiding light, illuminating the path toward inner healing and restoration. If you find yourself standing at the crossroads of pain and uncertainty, contemplating whether professional help is the right choice, take a moment and acknowledge the courage it takes to reach out. Seeking therapy or counselling is not a sign of weakness but a testament to your strength and willingness to invest in your well-being.

Therapy provides a safe space, a sanctuary where you can freely express your emotions, thoughts, and concerns without judgment. A trained therapist or counsellor can become your trusted confidant, a compassionate ally who walks beside you on this healing journey.

Within the therapeutic space, you are given the opportunity to explore the complexities of your thoughts and feelings with a professional equipped with the tools to guide you through the inner healing process. They are skilled in navigating emotional turbulence, providing insights and strategies tailored to your unique circumstances.

Therapy or counselling offers a multifaceted approach to inner healing. It may involve individual sessions, where you have the opportunity to delve deep into your own emotions, fears, and hopes. In these sessions, the therapist can help you unravel the intricate layers of pain and betrayal, offering guidance and support as you navigate the labyrinth of healing.

Additionally, therapy can be immensely valuable for rebuilding trust and reconnecting with the cause of your wounds. It provides a neutral ground for open communication, fostering a safe environment to express vulnerabilities, fears, and desires. A skilled therapist can facilitate constructive conversations, guiding toward understanding, empathy, and, ultimately, healing. You will become strong enough to embrace imperfection from the emotional pain and disappointments that come with emotional wounds.

Through the therapeutic process, you will gain invaluable insights and practical tools to navigate the complex emotions that arise after the hurts and pain. You will learn effective communication techniques, coping strategies, and ways to rebuild and restore. The journey may not always be easy, but with the guidance of a professional, you will have the support needed to navigate the challenges.

Seeking professional help does not imply that you are broken beyond repair. On the contrary, it signifies your commitment to growth, resilience, and the belief that inner healing is possible. It is a testament to your dedication to rebuilding a foundation of trust and creating a future filled with love, connection, and renewed hope.

Allow yourself the gift of professional guidance, knowing that you are taking an essential step toward inner healing and embracing the possibility of a brighter future. You deserve healing, and with the support of a skilled professional, you can navigate the complexities of emotional pain, reclaim your strength, rewrite the narrative of your future and embrace imperfection from your hurts.

As we reach the end of this chapter on inner healing, we reflect upon the transformative journey we have embarked on. We have explored the complex emotional impact that follows emotional wounds, acknowledging the rollercoaster of emotions arising from how we see ourselves or what people have done to us. In our exploration, we have discovered empowering strategies and tools to rebuild ourselves and navigate growth with grace and resilience.

Inner healing has been at the core focus of our emotional wounds. We have delved into effective communication techniques, learning to navigate difficult conversations with empathy and understanding. Through these heartfelt exchanges, we have begun to rebuild the emotional connection that was once shattered. We have also embraced the importance of establishing boundaries and relationship agreements, creating a foundation of trust and accountability for the future.

Throughout this chapter, we have not shied away from the intense pain emotional wounds bring. We have allowed ourselves to process and express these emotions, understanding that inner healing comes through acknowledging and working through the pain. Self-care and self-reflection have played pivotal roles in our journey, as we have prioritized our well-being and embarked on a path of self-discovery. We have recognized the value of seeking professional help, knowing that therapy or counselling can provide guidance and support as we navigate the complexities of healing.

Rebuilding self-trust has been a profound aspect of our journey. We have diligently restored confidence and belief in our judgment and instincts. Through self-reflection and growth, we have embraced the truth that our worth is not defined by the actions of others or what we think of ourselves but by our resilience and capacity for growth.

As we conclude this chapter, we do so with hope and optimism. We have learned that inner healing is a process that takes time and dedication, but it is possible to move forward with a renewed sense of trust and connection. We may choose to rebuild ourselves, foster deeper connections with others, or find ourselves on a path of separation and growth, discovering new aspects of ourselves.

Remember that you possess the strength and resilience to heal from the emotional wounds of emotional wounds. By embracing the strategies and tools we have explored, you can rebuild and restore your emotional well-being and embrace a future filled with love, joy, and growth. The journey may be challenging, but it is through these challenges that we find our true strength and potential. You deserve happiness and fulfillment, and as you move forward, may you find solace in the knowledge that you can create a bright and thriving future.

CONCLUSION

In this book, *"Embrace Imperfections,"* we embarked on an awe-inspiring journey into understanding that our flaws, mistakes, wrongdoing, bad choices and all the damaging mishaps do not determine our future. We have discovered our incredible potential to change and adapt throughout our lives. We delved into the profound impact we can make by understanding the strengths of imperfections, using them to fertilize our future and support others who may be hurt. *"Embrace Imperfections"* are the neural pathways we can have on our overall well-being and happiness.

We have learned that we can reclaim the power taken from us. Our brains are not fixed entities but relatively malleable and capable of being reshaped if we can tap into the power of resiliency. Armed with this knowledge, we explored having a positive mindset and reconnecting with ourselves. There were various techniques and exercises to condition our minds and challenge ourselves, paving the way for personal growth and self-transformation.

We emphasized the importance of inner healing, realizing that we can choose our mental narratives and direct the course of our lives. Through dedicated practice, we can master our minds, developing mental toughness that enables us to overcome obstacles and face adversity with resilience. We can reconnect with ourselves and find peace.

A significant aspect of this journey involved mastering our emotions and cultivating positivity. We discovered the profound impact of our emotional wounds and the coping strategies that are considered evidence-based. By gaining a deeper understanding of these facets of our consciousness, we empower ourselves to make choices that align with our values and aspirations, fostering personal growth and fulfilment.

Furthermore, we recognized the critical role of feeding and fuelling our brains in optimizing their performance as we embrace our imperfections. We explored the significance of self-destructive behaviour and how it affects us neurologically.

We have laid the foundation for reconnecting with ourselves, armed with the knowledge of practical strategies to condition our minds and cultivate positivity. Our journey has taken us deeper into the realms of embracing our imperfections. We were able to see the light of how we can use our negative past to become fertilizers to help others grow. We have explored the immense potential of our minds and uncovered the tools and techniques to create lasting positive change.

With dedication, perseverance, and a commitment to personal growth, we have learned our capability to embrace our imperfections and transcend the limitations of negativity. The transformative has propelled us toward a brighter and more fulfilling future, where we become the architects of our happiness.

We also delved into the intricate landscape of emotions and their power over our thoughts and actions. We have embarked on a profound exploration of mastering our emotions and cultivating resilience, equipping ourselves with invaluable tools to navigate life's challenges with grace and strength.

Understanding the intricate workings of our minds, we have learned to recognize and acknowledge our feelings, embracing them as essential messengers guiding us through our experiences. By developing emotional intelligence, we have gained the ability to navigate the depths of our emotions with compassion and wisdom, allowing us to respond thoughtfully rather than impulsively.

Through a series of exercises and practices, we have honed our skills in emotional regulation, enabling us to manage and channel our emotions in healthy and constructive ways. We have discovered the importance of self-care and self-compassion, recognizing that tending to our emotional well-being is crucial for embracing imperfections and maintaining a positive mindset.

Central to our journey was cultivating resilience—the ability to bounce back from setbacks, adapt to change, and thrive in adversity. We have explored the power of a growth mindset, embracing challenges as opportunities for growth and learning. By reframing our setbacks as stepping stones toward personal development, we have harnessed the strength to persevere and rise above obstacles.

We also recognized the significance of cultivating positive relationships and a strong support network we need to *"Embrace Imperfections."* Through connections with others, we found solace, encouragement, and the inspiration to stay resilient in life's trials. Building a resilient mindset involves individual effort and seeking and providing support within our communities.

We have also explored our journey of self-transformation and embracing positivity nears its culmination. We explored the fascinating realm of hurts that have been locked or not dealt with from the past: memories and their profound influence on our thoughts, beliefs, and overall well-being. We have delved into cultivating new memories and harnessing their power to shape our mindset and perception of the world, using our imperfections to better ourselves.

By understanding the intricate workings of memory formation and recall, we have learned to unveil the remarkable ability to reshape past negative experiences and reinterpret their meaning. This is an indicator of embracing the imperfections and moving ahead. We have gained the knowledge of recognizing the internal power we carry. We must let go of limiting beliefs hindering our growth and embrace empowering ourselves.

Through practical exercises and techniques, we harnessed the capacity to fertilize our future from the dung of our past. By consciously choosing to focus on moments of joy, gratitude, and accomplishment, we embrace imperfections to naturally gravitate towards optimism and resilience. We have witnessed the transformative impact of fostering a positive mindset as it rippled through our thoughts, emotions, and actions, leading to greater well-being and fulfilment.

Moreover, we have deepened our understanding of the interconnectedness between our thoughts, emotions, and memories affected by wrong choices, weaknesses, and regrets. We recognize that our mental and emotional states influence the encoding and retrieval of memories, and in turn, our memories shape our perceptions and beliefs. By intentionally nurturing positive thoughts and emotions, we created a virtuous cycle where positive memories reinforce positivity, fuelling our journey of self-transformation. We need to remind ourselves that our past does not determine our future.

As we conclude this transformative book, "Embrace Imperfections," we celebrate our progress in cultivating a transformed mindset and embracing the power to change our past. We can unlock the potential within us to create lasting change and lead fulfilling lives.

However, this is not the end of our path. It is an invitation to embrace a lifelong commitment to self-growth and positivity. Our brains continue to evolve and adapt throughout our lives. The journey of embracing imperfections is an ongoing process, requiring consistent effort and dedication.

Let us carry the lessons learned and the tools acquired from this book as we navigate the vast landscape of our minds. May we remain steadfast in our commitment to reclaim power personal power, reconnect with ourselves, embrace imperfections, have purpose and meaning, carry a positive mindset, do away with self-destructive behaviours, create coping strategies for emotional wounds, fertilize our future with our negative past and focus on inner healing.

By embracing imperfections, we elevate our lives and become beacons of positivity, radiating inspiration and hope to those around us. Together, let us create a ripple effect of positivity and transformation, reshaping our world.

Thank you for joining me on this transformative journey of "Embrace Imperfections." May your understanding carry you further in life to bring healing to your wounded heart and soul. As you put closure to your past and embrace your future, you will soon realize your past does not define your future.

The End!

www.ingramcontent.com/pod-product-compliance
Lightning Source LLC
Chambersburg PA
CBHW031126020426

42333CB00012B/256